You're Invited

AN UNFILTERED GUIDE

TO BEING A BRIDE

Weddiculous

JAMIE LEE

WITH JACQUELINE NOVAK

HarperOne
An Imprint of HarperCollinsPublishers

HarperOne

FIRST EDITION

Designed by Janet Evans-Scanlon

Library of Congress Cataloging-in-Publication Data has been applied for.

ISBN 978–0–06–245560–4

16 17 18 19 20   LSC/H   10 9 8 7 6 5 4 3 2 1

CONTENTS

SMILE FOR THE CAMERA!

You're Engaged!

OMG! wenza weddin?

WOWOWOW. CONGRATULATIONS!! YAYYYYY! YOU'RE GETTING *married. How'd he propose? Were you surprised? Shocked? Did you literally fall over from shock? Did you hit your head when you fell? That's the most romantic way to get a concussion!!!! Wenza wedding? Big or small? What are you thinking? Hometown or here? Will it be black tie and do I get a plus one? Again: Congratulations!!!!!!!!! I would type more exclamation points, but my carpal tunnel is kicking in from hyper-enthusiastic texting!!! Ouch, my hands.*

This is the gist of messages I got from friends and fam when I announced I was engaged. It immediately became about the wedding. As in, the day itself, rather than the lifetime commitment. I don't know what I expected: Were they supposed to ask me about how this engagement affects the subtleties of my dynamic with boyfriend, now fiancé, Dan?

But still. The instant, alarmingly specific questions about everything from menu to venue felt like a pop quiz. All of a sudden, the second the ring's on the finger, the clock starts ticking, and then someone says, "Pencils up," and "By the way, this test is gonna cost you a lot of money."

This is when you might start cracking semi-serious jokes about eloping.

Let me say now: Eloping is fine for some.

But you're not eloping.

You picked up this book because, when you got engaged, you were so excited you bought yourself a huge iced coffee and made a beeline for the nearest Barnes & Noble and spent the next seven hours there until security kicked you out. You yelled, "Only fascists close at ten o'clock on a Monday!" as they locked the doors on you, and now you're banned from that location. Okay, maybe that's just me. In any case, I knew I wanted to plan a wedding. Or rather, I didn't consider the alternative, i.e., NOT planning. Little did I know what I was in for. But I made it through. I found the dress, I figured out the guest list, and I danced my ass off at the end of the night. And I'm here now to bestow my glorious wisdom onto you.

This is a bride's book, from bride to bride. If you're *not* a bride, you're reading *Weddiculous* because:

- You've entertained the idea of engagement and plan to leave this book out so your partner sees it and gets a motherfucking clue.
- You never want to plan a wedding, or had one and hated it, and want to laugh at my pain.
- There's cake on the cover, and you like cake.

Welcome, friends! Unlike a wedding planner or a bridal magazine, I won't be guarded, delicate, or talk around things. Wedding planners' advice always comes around to you buying more services, for which they take a commission. Bridal mags are so afraid of being real because it might destroy the fantasy, and fantasy is what they're selling. Not me! I'm just a bride willing to lay it out to you straight.

Time to take your first vow:

I vow to banish from my lips any mentions of eloping, half-joking mentions, or melodramatic shrieks such as "We should just elope" or "We're fucking eloping!" . . . including any euphemisms such as "running off to Vegas" or "going to city hall."

NOW WE CAN BEGIN.

YOU'RE ENGAGED AF!
now what?

IF YOU'RE ANYTHING LIKE ME WHEN NEWLY RINGED UP, YOU leap at the chance to finally have an excuse to pick up the $75 quarterly issue of *The Knot* along with the most recent issue of *Modern Bride*, *Southern Bride*, *Northern Bride*, and whatever other regional market you fit into (I'm looking at you, *Swamp Bride*). I call this group "Big Bridal," and it includes all the bullying voices that make up the bridal industry and even the bloggers who've fallen under their sway, echoing the sentiment that if you don't make your wedding unforgettable, you've failed.

These publications have been the only guidance available about how to handle the wedding planning process (until now). You weigh yourself down, compromising your posture, which is already suffering from the fact that you travel with a duffel bag instead of a roll-on because the gate agents somehow allow those on board no matter how giant they are. Again, maybe it's just me. But after reading enough of these magazines, I started to laugh at them. They are so serious, so fear-based: "7 Ways to Make Your Wedding Stand Out!"; "4 Color Palettes Nobody Has Used Yet!"; "3 Passed Appetizers That Will Make Guests Scream 'My Palate Has Never Felt So Fucking Alive!'" The takeaway is always "If I don't shock, surprise, and downright dazzle guests with unexpected details, my wedding will be as embarrassing as audibly queefing at a funeral." If I don't get ornate candelabras for every table, even though I really just want to spend money on a great DJ, my tables will look as bleak as a Wendy's drive-thru on Christmas. In sum, "If I Don't Do X and Y, then Z (My Wedding) Will Suck."

This is how I really feel about weddings: They are goofy. Wonderful because they get everyone together, but stressful in ways that are not worth it in my opinion. They are also not mandatory. We seem to act as if they are, but they're not. They're volunteer work: If you're passionate about having one, have one! If you're not passionate about having one, find something you are passionate about and put effort into that! Marbling paper? Strengthening your core? Staring at the wall so long you hallucinate a portal to another dimension? Do it up!

Weddings are like a less creepy child beauty pageant. You're in a foofy dress, you're the JonBenét (but less sad), and a bunch of parents are gawking at you as you twirl and smile, and it feels nice to have that attention . . . but if you weren't in the pageant, you'd also be fine. You would just be a kid. And that's okay, too. Better, even. Because then you just get to be you.

So by all means—enter yourself in the pageant, but pull a *Little Miss Sunshine* and dance crazy and forget about winning or perfection. The stakes are low! You're just a kid, remember? Life goes back to normal after the pageant anyway. You can run through the sprinkler in the front yard and laugh about how uncomfortable that teeth-whitening procedure was, holy shit . . .

Don't get me wrong, it's not always going to be easy. Doing comedy and writing this book are the only things that kept me sane during the WPP (Wedding Planning Process.) To be honest, it was mostly nightmarish—with the exception of the event itself and the days leading up to the event, and the days immediately after. But the year and a half of planning was truly awful. Dan and I hated each other, I hated his family, my family hated whatever I hated, and, instead of working together in harmony, like a soon-to-be MARRIED COUPLE, we were playing for two different teams: The Lees vs. The In-Laws. Emotions were heightened due to stress from "too many cooks" weighing in on decisions, so what might have been "mild irritation" on a normal, non-pre-wedding day, felt like full-blown unforgiving disgust. But apparently this is not unique!

A few months before I got married, I met up with my friend Matt, a guy I worked with at my first writing job, for coffee and a platonic hug. I was wearing no makeup and an oil-stained hoodie because at that point I had no energy to expend towards anything other than staring at Excel documents and fighting with Dan—about money or the way he was raised or I was raised—throwing the word "divorce" around before we were even married.

Matt was the only person I knew who openly admitted to having an unsteady engagement to his now-wife Rosie. He said, and I quote, "Jamie, if you can get through your engagement, you can get through anything." I had never heard more comforting words. He said, "My wife and I almost split up while we were engaged. Multiple times. It's a complicated time in your life that everyone says is supposed to be the best time in your life. My wife was fighting with my mother, my mother would call me, crying . . . and the worst part is, I understood both of their points of view, so I couldn't side with either one of them. And of course that made my future wife livid."

I love my in-laws, and I am grateful for marrying into a family I can actually talk to and have a relationship with. My mother-in-law is one of the only people I enjoy speaking to on the phone, and maybe hands down the best listener I've ever met. I can call her with any problem, and she takes it on as her own. The woman cares. She loves. I am very lucky. Nevertheless, as is not uncommon, during the Wedding Planning Process, all I could think was "Everyone who is not my own mother or father, or therapist, leave me the fuck alone and let me find my own way. I am bride, hear me roar."

I'm not saying a rocky scenario will occur during your WPP. Maybe your stress will come from a more manageable, less personal source, like the cake baker suddenly quitting to become a surf instructor. Who's going to sculpt leaves out of fondant now that Dale's one with the tide?! Things will happen, whether it's emotional or familial or vendor-related. But you do not have to handle it alone.

That's why I'm writing this book. We need to have REAL TALK about just how fun/horrible/fabulous/repulsive/barf-inducing/great weddings and wedding planning can be. And how strange the concept of marriage is, and why we're still doing it. "Is it *okay* to have doubts?" Duh. Yes. "Is it *okay* to be scared?" Of course. You should be. It's scary. Wedding planning is *The Conjuring* for Basic Bitches. And marriage itself is *The Shining:* Terrifying, but also a well-respected classic.

I didn't grow up dreaming about my wedding. I never even made my Barbies get married. I just removed their Velcro halter dresses and made them bump plastic crotch delineations out of wedlock. I was very progressive like that. But if your wedding is something you've been plotting since you were little, or, if you're like me, since you first joined Pinterest, I'm here to ask you to set aside the road map of how everything is supposed to go, and get joyfully lost in the way things do go.

Wedding planning is less like a point-A-to-point-B commute from work. It is more like Waze: You'll be zipping down side streets, short-cutting through alleyways, giving a bratty teenager the finger for cutting you off, only to realize it's an old lady who can't see over the steering wheel. It could get ugly, but as on any harrowing journey, lessons will be gleaned. Get ready to learn a lot about yourself, your family, and your partner. But mostly your family and your partner, because it's easier to judge others than it is yourself.

What to Expect

In this book, I'll be covering rings, relatives, and ridiculously tiny crostini, often using alliteration to organize my thoughts. Not an exhaustive blanketing of topics based on years of wedding planning experience, because this was my first time. Instead, you'll be joining me as I fly by the seat of my yoga pants through my own wedding planning, shouting advice and anxieties, as I hurtle towards my wedding date on a tattered *Real Simple: Bridal Edition* as my magic carpet. You'll hear what I thought during the process and what insights I've had since. They both have their merits.

Hopefully, this book will guide you along but also give you a breather from the overwhelming taskmasters and super stressful list-makers over at bridal magazines and sites. Most wedding guides I've flipped through send me into a paralyzing panic about all the bullshit I have to take care of if I want my "big day" to be everything it should be. If I keep you from going bat-shit during this process, or make you feel better when you do, then I've given back to the temporary community of brides-to-be. This is the most important community service I've ever done, except for that time in ninth grade when I handed out Kashi bars at a Breast Cancer 5K to make my ex-boyfriend think I was a "good person."

Ultimately, it'll be up to you how seriously to take one of my amazing tips, like, "Hire a bartender with one working arm to shame guests out of bitching about long lines for drinks at the cocktail hour." I will say that I've seen that strategy work incredibly well, and I do recommend it.

So, shall we surrender to the planning of an archaic tradition and still have some fun?

But First: Are You Equipped to Plan a Wedding?

Trick question—no one is, and it's not a requirement anyway.

What you want to do is harness your enthusiasm, in whatever form it takes. Embrace the opportunity! Is it pathetic to throw yourself full throttle into planning because you are genuinely stoked to plan an event? Absolutely not. This is your time to shine, baby! Shine bright like a lightbulb!

(I refuse to fully quote). Just make sure you are doing it for the right reasons: It's an amusing extracurricular that directly ties into a celebration of you and your soon-to-be partner and marriage.

It's going to be easy to lose sight of that, but armed with this book, you'll have a much better chance. As your unofficial therapist, and official BBFF (Book Best Friend Forever), here is a quick inkblot test to assess your emotional capacity for wedding planning. Look at this image:

IF YOU SEE ANY OF THE FOLLOWING THINGS, YOU'RE IN THE CLEAR:

- ☐ A cruel, cruel hog
- ☐ A face with wings
- ☐ A man opening his coat
- ☐ A man standing between two dogs in profile
- ☐ An alien vagina dentata
- ☐ The lungs from the Bodies Exhibit
- ☐ A crab
- ☐ A four-eyed fox

IF YOU SEE ANY OF THE FOLLOWING THINGS, YOU'RE IN THE RED:

- ☐ Your dad never calling you back
- ☐ A bag of rotting Cheetos
- ☐ A child covered in superglue shouting, "My head is my prison!"
- ☐ Any senator
- ☐ A hot guy with one long fingernail, i.e., Cocaine Pinky
- ☐ Katherine Heigl
- ☐ Gluten

While there are no prerequisites, there is a lot to learn as you dive into Wedding World. Start with these handy repurposed acronyms:

BAE: Be Apologetic Endlessly. Great way to counteract the bridezilla label.

IRL: I'm Really Late. Fun way to tell people you haven't gotten your period and might be pregnant before the wedding.

NBD: Not budging, dickhead. Your cousin wants to bring his kids because he's too cheap to get a sitter? It's a no-kids Saturday night wedding. "Why, though?" Because it just is. Not budging, dickhead.

TBH: Tender Butthead. That's 90 percent of everyone you'll deal with during your engagement. From the florist to your own parents to your own self. A bunch of well-meaning idiots.

SMH: So Much Help. This might be the only time in your life when people are genuinely psyched to help you—like it rewards them with brownie points, as if they're volunteering at a nursing home. Later on, "Hey friend, can you watch my baby while I go out?" will be met with "Sorry! I've got plans." It's back to HELP IS A BURDEN right after the big day. So use people around you. You, too, can be a user! Not of intravenous drugs, hopefully, but of people!

Luckily, whether deeply stable or in a psychological danger zone, we're moving forward anyway. No Bride Left Behind.

Remember:
Big Bridal Is Watching

The second you're engaged you will find yourself to be part of a target market. Suddenly, all of the businesses, magazines, and articles aimed at brides are also aimed at you! How strange. You're suddenly in with an elite group. Kind of like a support group, a really chic one, Repurposed Mason Jars Anonymous, and the twelve steps are all box steps so you seem more coordinated during your first dance.

At first the sheer number of "You're a bride—now what?" magazine articles and websites might feel like a warm embrace, saying, "Don't worry, someone's got all the answers—us!" But no one has all the answers. Big Bridal is an industry like anything else, and they're very convincing, tapping into deep fears and societal instincts, triggering a lot of shame and doubt. It's essential to take a step back and laugh at Big Bridal . . . or be consumed whole.

Consider the fact that bridal magazines started a thousand years ago when all the articles were about hiding polio legs under a wedding gown or how to propose to your first cousin. As each issue goes by, they have to think of more shit to write about, which means they have to convince you that there is a new thing to worry about. Remember, Martha Stewart is a criminal. A real one. She did time for insider trading, so believe me, she loses no sleep over making you feel like you should hire a calligrapher to address your wedding invitations.

Throughout the ensuing sections, I will be including sentiments I've come across from Big Bridal . . . as a point of comparison or a jumping-off point. When Big Bridal says "You must," I will say "Well, maybe."

Here are three examples of the Big Bridal style of advice. Let's assess.

BIG BRIDAL SAYS: **Focus on the big picture.**

I SAY: **Wait, how big?**

At first I thought they surely meant "Weddings ultimately don't matter, so have fun and do whatever you want!" No. What they mean is "As opposed to focusing on linens, focus on creating a vibe." I love how creating a vibe is what *The Knot* considers big picture. When someone tells you to focus on the big picture in life, it means "Stop living in your head. People are dying of AIDS! Women in third-world countries aren't allowed to give birth to baby girls because only sons are of value! Cancer is a killer!" It doesn't mean "Don't think about napkin rings. Think about what the napkin rings SAY about you and your fiancé. If they are silver, that's a cooler tone than gold. Are you guys warm like gold or cool like new parents who live in Brooklyn?" The word "big" typically means . . . big. But in bridal speak, big picture just means slightly less insanely small picture! How confusing.

BIG BRIDAL SAYS: Learn wedding etiquette and then listen to the small, still voice within to decide if you want to be the type of pig who disobeys it.

I SAY: There's no proper wedding etiquette other than BE CONSIDERATE OF OTHERS AND YOURSELF.

You are not obligated to do anything you don't want to do, but being mindful is a good guiding tool in life, so it works the same in weddings. We are conditioned to believe that there are certain things we MUST do, but when you remember that weddings themselves are optional, suddenly the concept of Weddiquette holds less weight.

BIG BRIDAL SAYS: Don't sweat the small stuff . . . definitely worry about the small stuff but don't sweat, because you're ugly when you sweat.

I SAY: Also do not sweat the big stuff.

My friends had a tornado hit their wedding in Austin. The outdoor tent fell on us and the majority of the guests. It was mayhem. However, the cool thing is, my friends look back on that day just as fondly as they would if there had been perfect sunny weather. Again: Existential crisis talk or a helpful mantra? You decide! Now repeat after me:

I will break free of The Knot and other institutions of its ilk, or I will form a healthy relationship with it, in which I recognize its endless materials are a playground, not a school.

"CARE" VS. CARE:
your 'tude going in

BIG BRIDAL SAYS: **Every single detail matters.**

I SAY: **Every single thing you say sounds extreme.**

AS MUCH AS I FIND WEDDING CULTURE FASCINATING AND looked forward to checking off all of the boxes, like getting the dress, hearing speeches at the rehearsal dinner, etc., I realize how silly this all seems. Weddings are kind of dumb. Getting your families and friends together? Not dumb at all. Awesome, in fact. Saying vows in front of them? A little old-fashioned but also awesome. Having a party to celebrate you and your main squeeze? Werk, werk, werk. But everything else is just fun and dumb, details to obsess over because it's exciting to make a task out of sifting through photographs of elaborately decorated cakes on *The Knot* while delighting in a *Gilmore Girls* binge sesh, even though you have to keep pausing and rewinding so you don't miss one of Lorelai's signature quips. Modern wedding planning is all about intentionally making mountains out of molehills. They'll call it "being detail oriented."

But there's an important distinction to make: I really don't *care*—in my soul, in the depths of my brain. I am *choosing* to care. I am not a victim of my wedding; nobody should be. But a lot of women are. Your wedding is not your boss or your professor or your prison guard or anyone else who has authority over you. Don't give it that kind of power. Because at the end of the day, you are volunteering to have one.

And that's precisely why it's fun. You can care about the wedding without *caring*. Meaning, you can make choices about little details because those choices are fun, there is no right or wrong, the stakes are low, and anyone who judges you for your choice is as insecure as that middle school bully, whose home life was likely horrific and who probably needed your help.

So it is exciting to "care." But to CARE, to actually have emotional attachment to the invitations coming out a slightly darker shade of purple, to be upset that the cake arrived an hour late even though the ceremony isn't for another four hours, to be upset that one of your bridesmaids got a dress that was dark navy when you specifically said black and gave her the FREEDOM, the GIFT, to choose her own dress . . . None of it matters.

HERE IS WHAT MATTERS:

- You love your partner, and your partner loves you.
- That's it.
- And even if your ideas about love feel f'd up, and you could be making a terrible mistake, can you really call it a failure when it's the habit of, like, half the population to marry and divorce? It's actually the norm. Maybe you should feel like a crazy misfit if you don't end up divorcing.

Marriage is frightening; at least for me it is. My parents yell a lot and sleep in separate bedrooms, so I often asked myself, "What the hell am I doing getting married???" Almost to the point where someone would congratulate me on the engagement and I'd think, "Congrats on saying 'bye' to freedom?"

Yes, in some ways you are saying "bye," but try to focus on the fact that you will have a partner-in-crime and best friend for life. That is a huge gain. I'm an only child, so when I was a kid, I would always have to schedule playdates because I didn't have a sibling—a built-in, live-in playmate. But now I do! I have a perma-buddy! And that's way more important than the event that honors it. Remember to separate the wedding from the marriage. Especially as you plan the wedding. It helps keep stuff in check.

Let me paint a little picture for you. I went to a wonderfully wacky arts magnet high school in Dallas, Texas, called Booker T. Washington High School for the Performing and Visual Arts. We didn't have sports teams or even P.E. because all of our extracurriculars were art classes. (The most physical activity we engaged in was working a loom in textile class. You can really break a sweat weaving!) Whenever I would start a new art project, specifically a sculpture, it never fully turned out the way I had envisioned. Even as the artist, there was only so much control I had over the outcome. The finished product was never disappointing, though. In fact, it was thrilling to see something I shaped and built from the ground up in its complete form. It was like a birthing a child

A MIDSUMMER HETERONORMATIVE NIGHT'S DREAM

A wedding like the kind I've been planning is one big heteronormative clusterfuck. It runs through every ritual, and every tradition, every assumption about a *bride* and a *groom*. It's old-fashioned and I don't endorse it. However, instead of making this a manifesto about the ass-backwardness of mainstream wedding culture (which *should* be a book—someone write it!), I can only speak from my perspective, unhinged, and hopefully guide you even if your situation is not exactly like mine. I'll trust you to take from it what you can. I'm like a grandma who isn't changing her offensive references, but maybe has a few kernels of wisdom buried inside her tainted monologue?

and getting to say, "Oh, so *this* is what this thing looks like! Cool!" That's how I feel about planning a wedding. At a certain point you've gotta let the wedding "do its thing." And anything that goes wrong, isn't "wrong," it's just what it became, what it is.

Weddings are essentially a creative outlet where you get to express yourself (and your husband, I guess, but mostly you) through FOOD and DECORATIONS and MUSIC and CLOTHES and COLORS. Pretty much every platform you could ever creatively express yourself through, this is the one day you get to do it. So if you approach it like an art project, you might keep some of your sanity.

If you find that your wedding has become the boss of you and that you will be 9/11-style devastated if it doesn't come out exactly how you wanted it to, then something is wrong and it *isn't* your wedding. It is you. But you know what's comforting about it being you? You *can* control *you*.

Getting Started

RUNNING OUT OF TIME... line

OF COURSE EVERY WEBSITE AND MAG SAYS YOU MUST BE ON a strict schedule leading up to the wedding—making you feel like a failure if you don't stay on track. I would feel bad not providing the gospel of timelines because then you'd have to go look at *The Knot* to find it, and you might never make it out alive. So I've listed the Big Bridal approach each step of the way below, but I will be juxtaposing it with my perspective, giving you my own adjustments, interpretations, and musings.

> **BIG BRIDAL SAYS:** Print out the calendar we created so you know when you should start chastising yourself for not having done something yet.
>
> I SAY: If you're a calendar person, go nuts. Otherwise, just allow your last-minute nature to make decision making easier (there are fewer dress options when there's no time to get them tailored).

BIG BRIDAL SAYS:

- Think about the type of wedding you want and draw up a budget.

- Assemble a "planning team." Maybe hire a wedding consultant?

- Select several viable wedding dates, then check with your venues, officiant, and important guests before finalizing.

- Ask people to be in your wedding party.

- Where will your ceremony be? Where will your reception be?

- Optional: Have an engagement party. You may want to register beforehand for gifts.

I SAY:

- A wedding "consultant" is the same as a planner. It sounds like another person to hire in addition to the planner. It's not.

- I did not ask anybody to be in my wedding party at this time. I had tension with a best friend whom I wanted to be my bridesmaid. There was distance there, so I wanted to defer this selection process as long as possible. Also at this time, I thought my wedding was going to be in New York, when it ended up being in Simi Valley, California. Twelve months out is far out. Relax. Also, I didn't have an engagement party, and I certainly was not registered.

THEY FORGOT

- Consider hiring a friend in Charleston to plan the wedding just to have someone other than your family involved—a neutral party.

- Have your fiancé's whole family gang up on you and tell you that you're crazy for asserting yourself because they know how to do weddings (your fiancé's dad is a wedding photographer).

- Get bullied into using Rupert, the flower guy (more on him later . . .), even though his version of a "good deal" was $12K on ficus plants to make the indoor venue feel "outdoors-y."

- Get a puppy. Name him Dennis.

BIG BRIDAL SAYS:

I SAY:

- Get your wedding dress!
- What kind of food do you want to serve? Thai fusion? Steak? Upscale comfort?
- Decide what type of entertainment you want. A jazz pianist, violinists, a DJ or band?
- Think about your floral options.
- Research and book your wedding professionals. Interview vendors: photographer, videographer, reception band or DJ, and florist.
- Register for gifts.
- Contact rental companies if you need to rent anything for the ceremony or reception, such as a tent or extra chairs.

- I like the use of the terms "think about" and "research" here because I could technically say I was on track while no concrete details had been figured out at all. At this point, you should probably know when and where you're getting married. I (barely) did.

THEY FORGOT

- Ask Distant Best Friend (DBF) to be a bridesmaid, brushing your feelings under the rug so as to avoid (more) conflict in your life because you are very, very mature.
- Start questioning your fiancé's upbringing (coddled middle child) and have him start questioning the way you were raised (coddled only child).
- Take a girls' trip to New York City, look at dresses even though there are plenty of wonderful stores where you live. Frolic. NYC is great for frolicking.

BIG BRIDAL SAYS:

- Book ceremony musicians.
- Order bridesmaid dresses.
- Begin to plan your honeymoon!
- Send out save-the-date cards. Especially if you're getting married during a tourist or holiday season, or heading off to Puerto Rico for a destination affair!

I SAY:

- I sent save-the-dates five months out. Not six. I'm the worst. But everyone who was going to come still came. Nobody was like, "If I had only gotten this a month ago, I would have attended your wedding!"
- "Book ceremony musicians." If you have a band, your band will play the ceremony. It's part of the package. Also, why would you book the ceremony musician at a different time than the reception musician? It doesn't make sense.

THEY FORGOT

- Hit a breaking point where you decide to stop booking everything on your own and hire a planner. But at least you're realizing that there's a problem and that you need help.
- Attend couple's counseling to reach understanding about how to successfully merge families/not kill each other.

BIG BRIDAL SAYS:

- Order invitations and select wedding rings.
- Shop for men's formal wear.
- Renew or get passports, if necessary.
- Envision your wedding cake, and research, interview, and book a cake designer.

THEY FORGOT

- Supplement couple's counseling with individual sessions, on the phone or in person, to complement the progress being made together with mutually exclusive self-improvement. Feel free to recalculate your budget, because sanity can be expensive.
- Feel confused/hurt when DBF stays in a different hotel from the rest of the bachelorette party in Vegas (see details on page 203), but once again, do not confront her or your own feelings. Just passive-aggressively act weird to her the whole weekend because you are, you guessed it, very, very mature.

I SAY:

- Wedding cake design can be done two to three months out, and that's plenty of time. Below you will see "order a wedding cake." That's the same exact thing as "booking a designer." You just go to a bakery, select a design from their book, taste different fillings, and put a deposit down. There's no official HIRING of a "designer." Stella McCartney isn't taking a break from her fashion empire to blend flour and butter. There's no "Frosting by Marc Jacobs." It's like any other cake bakery situation. You could probably order your cake a month out and be FINE.
- We didn't even think about a honeymoon other than fantasize about taking one in place of having a wedding. We knew we would do a minimoon post-wedding in Cabo, and then plan something bigger and farther away after the wedding, because I'm a horrible multitasker. I can barely talk on the phone while putting half-and-half in my coffee, let alone plan a wedding while coordinating a big trip. My hat, as well as my dress, undies, and bra, goes off to anyone who can do both simultaneously. I'm left naked and in awe of you.

BIG BRIDAL SAYS:

I SAY:

- You've selected a wedding cake. Now order it!

- Hire a calligrapher, if you want your invitations professionally addressed.

- Attend your shower. (It may be earlier, depending on when your hosts decide to have it.)

- Hire transportation for the wedding: limos, Escalades, a school bus. Look into transportation sooner if you're considering renting streetcars or over-the-top travel.

- It's hilarious that "attend your shower" is on the checklist. "Show up." CHECK.

THEY FORGOT

- Cry to your mom on the phone about your fiancé/in-laws.

- Cry to your aunt on the phone about your fiancé/in-laws.

- Cry to in-laws about DBF.

- This actually belongs in every part of the timeline from twelve months+ to two weeks before.

TWO MONTHS BEFORE

BIG BRIDAL SAYS:

I SAY:

- Write your vows.

- Purchase gifts for parents, attendants, and each other.

- Book a hair and makeup artist and go for a trial run.

- Write your vows? I did this *two days before my wedding.*

- If your birthday comes up before your wedding, give yourself the permission to lazily celebrate it, because your wedding is essentially a birthday party on steroids. The birthday before my wedding, I ate chicken wings, I played one round of mini golf, and then Dan and I went go-karting. (I made him drive. #lazy)

BIG BRIDAL SAYS:

I SAY:

- Apply for a marriage license. Check with the local bureau in the town where you'll wed.

- Bride: Have final gown fitting. Bring your maid of honor along to learn how to bustle your dress. Have the dress pressed and bring it home.

- Create a wedding program to hand out to guests.

- Order and plan in-room welcome baskets for out-of-town guests.

THEY FORGOT

- Receive text from cousin's girlfriend asking for them to be seated at a different table from my uncle, my dad's brother. When you call up dad to get the scoop, dad says that cousin might be mentally unstable—just seat them at the same table anyway.

- In the spirit of "things can't get any worse," call DBF to nervously declare all the ways you feel she has wronged you over the past year and a half. After two straight hours of hashing it out, have her generously ask how things are going with your fiancé's family. #RoadToRecovery #ShouldHaveTalkedToHerSooner

- I strongly encourage a fitting *a week and a half* before the wedding. I didn't lose any real weight until the last minute, so that fitting was crucial. And if you buy your dress at Neiman's, they will alter until the last minute and then overnight the dress to you. It's awesome.

- Wedding programs—NAH!

- I agree—get welcome bags done now. It takes longer than you think it will. Drive them to the hotel ASAP as well. It takes a while to explain who gets what, how many bags per room—especially if some bags contain different goodies from others. It's a process. Do not wait until right before your wedding. By the way, this is the only fearmongering I will do this entire book. Now back to your regularly scheduled chill programming.

BIG BRIDAL SAYS:

- Give caterer final guest head count. Include vendors, such as the band, who will expect a meal.

- Supply location manager with a list of vendor requests, such as a table for the DJ or setup space needed for a florist.

- Plan reception seating chart.

- Have your table and place cards, and all wedding paper, printed, or finalize list with the calligrapher you've hired.

- Give ceremony and reception site managers a schedule of vendor delivery and setup times, plus contact numbers.

- Groom: Get a haircut.

- Attend your bachelorette party!

I SAY:

- Do your bachelorette whenever. I did mine six months before, and there was no part of me that felt bummed it wasn't RIGHT before another HUGE event.

- The "location manager" and the caterer, and any other such people will probably e-mail or text asking for this info anyway. **Rely on them to come a-callin'.** It's like putting on your to-do list "hand in homework" when you can rest assured the teacher will remember to ask for it.

- Watch your mom and fiancé argue about rehearsal dinner calculations in front of you, while you bury your face in a pillow and pray to be teleported to a remote island with no moms or fiancés, only coconuts and a shaman named KoopKoop. And Dennis the dog. He can come, too.

BIG BRIDAL SAYS:	I SAY:

- Bride: Have your gown steamed.
- Groom: Go for a final tux fitting.
- Groom: Ask the best man and groomsmen to have final fittings to ensure that their suits fit properly.
- Determine wedding party positions during the processional and recessional parts of the ceremony.
- Confirm final details with each and every vendor. Discuss any necessary last-minute substitutions.
- Help guests figure out how to get to and from the airport or train station. Help coordinate transportation for them.
- Call rental company for pickup times and locations for the limousines.
- Deliver welcome baskets to the hotel concierge; include names and delivery instructions.

- This is where your personality is likely to take over. Not everyone's into "confirming details" with vendors. I love confirmations. But if you prefer to have faith, go for it.
- Have people figure out how they'll get from the airport or train station themselves. We're all adults with smart phones.

THEY FORGOT

- Start drinking.

DAY BEFORE

BIG BRIDAL SAYS:

I SAY:

- Provide your "wedding team" with an emergency phone number to call on the day of the wedding.

- Write checks and work out any final balances to be paid at the end of the reception.

- I hope they don't think I am that emergency contact. I'm the general of this army, and if you have a problem, I really need you to handle it yourself, Sergeant.

- Prepay when you can. Who wants to be writing out numbers as words in cursive on their wedding day?

THEY FORGOT

- Watch in-laws get a little verklempt when the bill comes out at the bar where everyone is hanging out. Relax and split it. At this point, what's another fifty bucks? #momoneymoproblems

NIGHT BEFORE

BIG BRIDAL SAYS:

I SAY:

- Rehearse ceremony. Have the wedding party, immediate family, and your officiant at the ceremony site to hammer out details.

- Give bridesmaids gifts, especially if they are wearing them the next day.

- Bring candles, yarmulkes, or any other ceremony accoutrement to the site.

- Go to your rehearsal dinner, if you decided to have one.

- Hauling a box of yarmulkes just doesn't feel like something I want to do the night before.

- Ugh, I need a personal assistant.

THEY FORGOT

- Feel completely weirded out by a bridesmaid's rehearsal dinner speech in which she seemed to be making a lot of "breakthroughs," the kind most prefer to do in private with a therapist.

BIG BRIDAL SAYS:

I SAY:

- Present parents and in-laws with gifts.

- Give best man the officiant's fee envelope, to be handed off after the ceremony.

- Introduce your reception site manager to your consultant or maid of honor for questions or problems during the reception.

- Hand off wedding bands to the best man and maid of honor to hold during the ceremony.

- Assign a family member or bridesmaid to be the photographer's contact so he or she knows who's who.

- Again with the gifts? Just tell them where the whiskey's at.

- Make your friend officiate for free. Cash hand-offs at the wedding feel a little crass, anyway. Can more wedding vendors get on board with app-based payment methods?

- Move all of the "Day of" tasks off your list. You won't have time, or even remember to do any of them, so just handle them the day before, or say fuck it.

THEY FORGOT

- ENJOY!!!!!!! It's your wedding day. What's with this long checklist?

BIG BRIDAL SAYS:

I SAY:

- Prearrange for someone to take charge of returning any rentals.

- Plan in advance for someone to take the bride's gown for cleaning, and return the groom's rented tux.

- Write thank-yous to guests who bought you a gift, and to any vendors who were especially helpful.

- They are telling us to do stuff after the wedding, but then they're telling us to have prearranged it. Not helpful.

- I likely won't be sending thank-you notes to vendors. I'm not here to network in the wedding industry. If you really blow me away with your work, I'll probably tearfully embrace you during the wedding night, saying, "You saved me." Otherwise, the dollars I spend on your services . . . fold them in half if you're desperate for a note.

THEY FORGOT

- DRINK and EAT A LOT. The day after my wedding I went to Malibu Country Mart with my matron of honor and her husband and had a double cheeseburger and fries, and that night I ate a whole roast chicken. Give back to your body. It went through a lot to look and feel pretty (i.e., stupidly thin and weak).

- Receive call from father happily reporting that my "unstable" cousin and my uncle are now on great terms because my wedding forced them to talk and smooth things over. Victory!

- Upon seeing your decorative gift receptacle emptier than you hoped, briefly panic that the cash envelopes were stolen, but then realize that a lot of people just didn't give you money . . . jerks.

I'm not encouraging you to slack off with wedding planning, but I am encouraging you to know that even if you did everything according to the Big Bridal timeline, you would still have plenty to freak out about. This timeline does not stop you from having constant worry. If anything, it adds to it because it makes you believe you need to be thinking about programs with the same weight and intensity as you think about MoH (maid of honor) gifts. You can pick and choose what to care about (see chart). You're allowed. Weddings are not objective. They're subjective. Therefore, do it your way. These are merely *guide*lines, not *dead*lines. The life you save may be your own.

PRIORITIZATION EXERCISE

Pick six. Focus on those. Allow yourself to pay less attention to the rest.

- Flowers
- Dress
- Reception food
- Entertainment (DJ, band)
- Photographer, videographer, photo booth
- Invitations
- Guest care (accommodations, transportation, gift bags)
- Cake
- Bachelorette party
- Bridal shower
- A "really special" ceremony
- Random add-ons that will make your heart sing (like a tattoo artist on hand)

MAKING IT OFFISH:
announcing you're engaged on social media

THE TIMELINE COUNTDOWN DOESN'T OFFICIALLY BEGIN UNTIL you announce your engagement to the world, by using the same apps you use to complain about your flight delay or show that you're eating brunch.

No shame in that game. It's easier than having to tell every single person you know when you run into them. Let them process the fact you're off the market—at home, alone, or with their shrink.

So post away, but first contemplate: How do you want your social media community to feel when they look at your photos? Unimpressed? Happy for you? Jealous and resentful?

TECHNICALLY A RING SHOT
BUT WAY TOO MUNDANE.

NICE, STRAIGHTFORWARD—NO ONE
CAN BE MAD AT THIS PIC.

ANNOYING. "WE GET IT. SOMEONE LOVES YOU
AND YOU'VE GOT THE RING TO PROVE IT."

PHOTO COMPOSITION TIPS THAT INSPIRE AND ABATE JEALOUSY SIMULTANEOUSLY

1. Rest your hand atop something that offsets the materialism. Make sure some charity leaflets are in focus beneath your hand—you want the picture to suggest that, yes, you have a diamond, and should you ever run out of money to give to charities, you would *of course* immediately sell the diamond. But until then . . . isn't it pretty?

2. Own the brag. Do not try to sneak that glorious diamond into some pic where you're trying to come off down-to-earth or saintly. No photos of your ringed hand fashioning a shoulder sling for a bird who tore its ACL.

3. Consider including in the background your broken-looking fiancé. He might actually be broke now, and people will appreciate seeing the cause and effect between the ring and the proposer.

4. Starbucks has the best lighting. It's sort of dim and sultry, so the dried-out scones look like SEXY dried-out scones, but it's just bright enough to show off your diamond's rainbow-prism powers. Grab a latte and a *latte** pics while you're in there.

5. Giving a shout-out to the jeweler with a picture of the ring box is a great excuse for posting about your ring a second time. (Kay's is just a little mom-n-pop shop, right?) Also, promoting businesses on Insta is very Reese Witherspoon. This is your chance to say "Thanks to Karen and the wonderful team at Cold Stone Stonery" or whatever, and to feel like a STAR. Using the word "team" is also very Reese, BTW.

---

* I'm sorry for the pun, but chai just had to! Are we still friends?

Budgetaboutit!

YOU'RE GETTING MARRIED? COOL, SO WHO'S PAYING? DISCUSSING money is about as comfortable as peeling off a pair of Lululemon pants after spin class with that one instructor who works you out so hard, you feel like you just lost your butt-virginity to a bike seat. Hopefully, this will be a painless process for you. For me, I think putting cigarettes out on my forearm would have been less painful.

> **BIG BRIDAL SAYS:** Our super scientific polling tells us that the average wedding costs $30–35K.
>
> **I SAY:** Okay, but who should pay what? Is it wrong to show up on my fiancé's parents' doorstep selling candy bars to give them the hint to cough up the g's?

It is crazy to spend $33K on anything that does not involve putting a roof over your head or trying to have a baby or putting your grown baby through college. That said, I set out to spend $45K on my wedding. From Dan's side, $20K, from my side, $25K, and whatever else I would provide because I'm the one who wins the bread in the family even though ironically I was off carbs for the wedding. Admitting the cost of our wedding, putting it on paper, makes me feel sick. I wish I had that money back. It's so much money. But I don't. It's gone. Poof. "Bye, money." "Bye, Jamie." (Wait, money CAN talk?)

I should also mention that there were different contribution styles within our wedding. My parents deposited their portion and had no interest in how it was being spent. Technically, I could have blown part of their share on a lifetime supply of flavored condoms, and they would not have known. Dan's family, on the other hand, wanted to know what their contribution was being put towards. There's a catch-22 to "everyone puts in the pot." Yes, there's a larger sum to work with, but family chipping in can mean "buying in," like the wedding is a time-share, an "equal say" democracy. Since brides are monarchs by nature, wanting to rule and dominate without the "townspeople" voting, this "Everybody has a voice!" shit can cause added anxiety.

When it was all said and done, our wedding cost about $60K. How did this happen? I'll tell you. The rehearsal dinner ended up being $6K. My mom was like, "Why do you need a rehearsal dinner?" We didn't. It was pleasurable and polite to our guests from out of town, and the caterer made an incredible ravioli that I fantasize about more than Justin Long telling me nervously but earnestly I'm "the one," but nobody

SHIT YOU DO NOT NEED

Paper invitations. Send them to old people who don't use e-mail (although my grandpa is ninety-four and has two accounts, so . . .). Otherwise, sorry, bitches. Here comes your Evite.

A wedding program. Another waste of paper and a waste of money. Forget it. Everyone knows what's happening. If they don't, they can ask a friend or make a doctor's appointment because maybe the 'shrooms they bought at Bonnaroo are having a lasting impact on their mental clarity.

Special linens. I was obsessed with upgrading to satin, and it just didn't matter. If the venue is nice, plain, white standard linens look fine. And if it's rustic, you might not need linens at all.

Upgraded glasses and silverware. Nobody cares. Catering upgrades, unless they are food related, are worthless.

would have faulted us for not having one. Above all, and this is going to sound positively psychotic, I viewed the rehearsal dinner as an opportunity for a "second dress." I didn't have the guts to do a costume change at the wedding, and wearing a white non-wedding dress the night before was built up in my head as something that needed to happen. I also fantasized about people making speeches to us. I wanted to see how I would be portrayed in a speech—would people play it safe and just compliment me, or would they rip me a new one? What kinds of friends do I have? Who will speak? These are questions I needed answers to, and apparently the price tag on such questions was $6K for me. Cool! JK.

There were other culprits, too: We had an after-party where we provided bar food. I just HAD to provide sangria and Moscow Mules as my signature drinks, with cute little names like "JamDan-gria" and "Marry Me Mule" . . . We had to have that band, which was, like, $7K—a DJ would have been $500 to $1K . . . I'm just reminiscing all the ways I could have saved . . .

Watch out, because you will likely hit a "fuck-it zone" closer to the wedding where you need problems solved, and it is worth more to just throw money at them than panic and add it to the roster of "And another thing that's gone wrong!" Things really add up towards the end. So come up with what you think is reasonable, and say it with me:

I vow to figure out how much I'm willing to spend on my wedding, and then lower that number by 20 percent, so that when I inevitably go over, I land somewhere close to what I originally wanted to spend.

CHOICES, CHOICES, drowning in choices

EVERY ASPECT OF WEDDING PLANNING IS A DECISION-MAKING challenge. And while my decision-making skills and maybe yours could use some improvement, wedding planning is stressful enough without having to add a regimen of increasing self-mastery.

> BIG BRIDAL SAYS: **Go on an exploratory mission through blogs, magazines, wedding fairs, and friends' photo albums and see what tickles your fancy.**
>
> I SAY: **Leave my fancy alone. Tickling is cruel.**

Decision-making stress began for me around the search for the wedding locale. We went back and forth a bunch. I have no decision-making strategies in place and neither does Dan. I cried and Dan comforted me. I drank coffee and stayed up late, weighing options, California versus New York. It was intense. Dan and I both have a bit of a location-identity crisis. It makes wedding planning very hard. I grew up in Texas; Dan grew up on Long Island. We technically met in LA, but our relationship didn't start until we both lived in New York. His parents are in New York. Mine are in Texas, but some of my family is in New Jersey and South Carolina. Dan and I live in LA, but we've only been here for a year. AHHHHH!

Even though I've never really dreamed of my wedding, I have dreamed of feeling dangerously chic on my wedding day, and it usually comes with a snowy New York City backdrop. And our dog, Dennis, could wear little white booties. Yes, California makes me feel chill but not gorgeous. New York romance and elegance is much more my speed. It just inherently feels more formal, and the temple we were looking at could be formal, but not stuffy formal, which is key to me. I'm all for people dressing up because it's fun, but having a cohesive, all-inclusive party vibe is more important to me. Then I thought, "California is great because it's beautiful and the weather is great and we could have it outdoors. Dennis could romp in the sand with an elegant white satin collar." Still, something in my heart was not stoked about it. I kept trying to shush that something. California was cheaper and easier because I fucking live here, but something about New York was calling to me.

Look at that paragraph. Imagine it on a loop in my head for weeks.

Then one day, a tsunami of relief rushed over me as the decision rolled out of my mouth. "It's New York." Dennis barked in approval. But he also barks a lot, so it's hard to say. I wondered if I was having one of those moments the magazines talk about where you "just know."

Shortly after, we had to decide on a date. Another fucking decision. December 5 or December 19? Back to the dry-erase drawing board. We called everyone in our families and obsessively polled friends: "Which date if you had to choose?" "The fifth?" "Why?" "I don't know." "So you hate the nineteenth?" "No, but I am starting to hate you." "Noted! Thanks!"

Doing a summer wedding in the heat wasn't me. I only want to sweat from anxiety during the hora chair tossing, not because half of the groomsmen are sporting pit stains through their tuxedo jackets in the photos. We decided on December 19.

Technically, we made that decision faster than the previous one. I suppose we were getting a little tiny bit better every day at swiftly making firm choices, much like Dennis's bowel movements, which ultimately firmed up, too.

See, Dennis had a stomach virus at the time and was shitting everywhere. Constantly having to stop my obsessive decision weighing to stoop down and spray and wipe away poop provided some useful grounding. Dog poop is one of the most grounding things there is. It literally requires you to look away from *The Knot*'s app on your phone to check where you're stepping.

Worse comes to worst, you change your mind because, news flash, it's *your* wedding. Yes, there are deposits and family annoyances to consider, but the sooner you can make *some* kind of decision, the sooner you can move on to more important things.

In the end we switched to California *and* changed the date. See what I mean? No decisions are final.

GET THE DUMP GOING

1. **Flip a coin for every decision and see how you feel when it determines one way or the other.** If you feel happy with the coin's choice, stick with it. If you feel upset, go the other way.

2. **Do a speed session.** Make ten decisions in ten seconds, and then stick with them for a week, without contemplation, and then see how you feel.

3. **Make one decision you hate on purpose.** If you feel as if a chalkboard table marker would ruin your wedding, choose that. It could be a good way to challenge yourself to realize that none of it really matters.

4. **Research the cost of hiring a wedding planner to make decisions for you.** Those rates will no doubt inspire you to do some old-fashioned, DIY decision making.

5. **Write up some draft e-mails to vendors or planners or friends stating your decisions.** Pretend you've made a choice even if you haven't. Once the e-mails are written, see if it might be less work to just hit send and get on with things, versus continuing to stew.

The Power of Taking a Decision Dump

While grossly inspired by Dennis's butt problems, "Decision Dump" is the best way I can describe what you need to do when you're constipated with possibilities.

You have a bunch of wedding-planning decisions to make, all of which you know will lead to totally different wedding vibes:

- What does this flower say about us as a couple?
- Since it is a winter wedding, should we do a hot-chocolate bar or an apple-cider bar?
- If we have the wedding in a ballroom, will we regret not having it in a loft?
- Are we loft people?!

The real truth is, you can't go wrong. There are no wrong decisions. There is only the feeling in the pit of your stomach created by not deciding. So decide! Poop out a choice! You'll feel so relieved.

But how? "I can't decide," you say. That's the thing. You're thinking of a decision as something that mystically floats up from within, or completely takes you over the way Patrick Swayze took over Whoopi's body in *Ghost*. No. It's actually just an action you take, like, say, the action of e-mailing the florist, saying, "Red flowers, please." It's a much better way to think of a decision.

I vow to make decisions happen, by taking actions on them, versus postponing action while I wait for decisions to make themselves known to me like oracle visions.

SEASONS: mother nature on her period

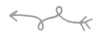

OH, THE TURNING OF OUR PLANET AROUND THE SUN AND ITS consequences. Suddenly you must contemplate what season speaks to you and for you and through you—it's like those quizzes (Which *Sex and the City* character are you? Which Disney princess is your left boob?), but with ramped-up financial consequences. Well, the only way *out* is *through,* so let's break it down.

> BIG BRIDAL SAYS: **What's your favorite season? What about your partner's? What?! You never asked?! Not impressed. Is there a type of precipitation that represents love to you? Soft rain? Then spring's your thing! Does snowfall scream divorce? Maybe! Philosophical quandaries of this kind really speed up the process of making decisions on appetizers and decor.**
>
> I SAY: **All seasons are equally annoying and wonderful.**

Remember the Decision Dump? Keep in mind the relief a decision will bring as we assess all these seasons, once, and never again. We shall get it out of our system here.

PROS:

- Snow is pretty.
- When it's cold, you want to snuggle harder.
- You can serve hot chocolate and apple cider. And eggnog!
- Maybe your guests can ski during the day?
- Mink stoles or just stoles in general. #stoles
- You don't even have to toy with the idea of an outdoor wedding. Everyone will be thrilled to hibernate inside with you.
- Flights might be cheaper in January after the holidays. Yay!
- Holidays!!! Oooh, oooh! If you have a December wedding, you can play Christmas music and nobody will think you're a lunatic who just loves slow-twerking to "Jingle Bell Rock."
- No thigh chafing in the cold, dry months.

CONS:

- It gets dark early, which can cause Seasonal Depression. In addition to the flip-flop basket by the dance floor, make sure you provide blankets for those who want to nap instead of dance.
- Will guests' flights be delayed due to weather? Or canceled?
- Ladies might have to wear stockings with their formal wear, which is always an awkward look. A gown with Wednesday Addams black tights? Still better than creepy '80s secretary panty hose.
- The event can't be outdoors. Even if you bring in heaters, you are a dick for scaring people pre-wedding that they will be freezing all night long.

FALL

PROS:	CONS:

- Weather is not too cold, but not too hot.

- Pumpkin shit is acceptable, encouraged, and expected.

- Even if you don't have pumpkins at your wedding, your guests can get a pumpkin latte at Starbucks the day of the wedding, which I'm pretty sure statistically increases endorphins. They'll be in a better mood.

- The leaves are turning! The leaves are turning! Ma! Pa! Look at the leaves!

- There's a vibe of apple picking even if it in NO way makes its way into your theme. It's just looming.

- Less thigh chafing, unless it's one of those hot Septembers.

- Venues are more expensive because this is prime time, in the world of weddings.

- Venues book up further in advance, which means you just can't set your heart on a particular place unless you are cool with a two-year (or more) engagement.

- Everyone has a wedding in the fall, which means people might not be able to make it because a friend they are even closer to has a wedding the same weekend.

PROS:

- Spring has a great reputation. It sounds dainty and lovely, with chirping birds aplenty.

- Not a lot of people have spring weddings, so there will be less competition.

- If it's outdoors, you can set up space heaters and people will think you're very thoughtful.

- Any style of wedding dress can work because this is a very "on the fence" season.

- Spring has a positive connotation. "New beginnings!"

- Flights are reasonable.

- The beginning of thigh chafing, unless that beaver sees its shadow.

CONS:

- No fun Starbucks drinks.

- Rain, sleet, sunshine, cloudy. Who the fuck knows? The weather is on its period.

- Wind. There's lots of wind. I hate wind. It makes your hair and your lip-gloss all chummy, and I'm very against their friendship.

- You still need a shawl or formal jacket if it's outside. Is there anything worse than having to accessorize a gown with a fucking coat or whatever? No. No, there is not.

PROS:

- School's out for summer.

- Warm weather, less rain.

- Gives your wedding a certain effortlessly chill vibe.

- You're not a bridezilla, you're a brideCHILLa . . .

- Your dress can be lighter weight, flowy, breezy.

- If it's indoors, guests will be psyched to get out of the heat.

- Simplicity is celebrated and condoned because everyone of every age will want to feel like they're ripped from the pages of an Abercrombie ad—carefree, skinny, tan, freckles on their noses, living in the moment, possibly with HPV? Who knows! Soak up the joie de vivre!

- Guests can go to the beach/lake during the day.

- Sweat equals . . . you guessed it, thigh chafing, giving guests an excuse to straddle the ice swan.

CONS:

- You knew this was coming: People will be sweating in their formal wear, which is the epitome of discomfort. Chiffon and pit stains? Ughhhh.

- Like the fall, a lot of venues book up in the summer. This could pose problems for your "dream wedding."

- Formality is harder to achieve in the summertime, just logistically. You want people to be comfortable because it's hot. Ever seen a linen tuxedo? You will.

- You might want a heavier ball gown and that just doesn't match up with the warm winds rolling through your outdoor vineyard venue.

- Guests might be sluggish due to beaching hard during the day.

- It gets dark so late. Tough to achieve the vibe of "some enchanted evening . . ." when the sun is still shining like an asshole.

Do you love your spouse only in a particular season? Hopefully not. Romance can live in any season, so fear not, your wedding can, too. There are no right choices, only the feeling of relief when a choice is made! This is an easy chance to practice the Decision Dump because it's really a choice between three options, since spring and fall are essentially interchangeable. Fall is just a slightly colder, less obnoxious spring. Fall is Kendall Jenner, spring is Kylie. Not a big difference. Most grandparents can't tell them apart.

VENUE:
where the party at?

BIG BRIDAL SAYS: Your venue says a lot about who you are.

I SAY: Your venue says, "This is where they chose to get married."

ULTIMATELY, THE PRACTICAL CONSIDERATIONS MATTER MORE than the representational. Consider the popular outside wedding with the reception under the tent. All the guests drive two hours to some farm that has one of the oldest houses in the country that you aren't allowed to go in. Please use the Porta Potties over the hill, thank you. It's a fun time that ends with people all going to a local motor inn for the night with a mason jar that has the bride and groom's initials painted on it. It's a wedding planner's version of going to class and seeing a substitute teacher. When a couple says they want the old "farm-and-mason-jar special," the planner's like, "Oh, I don't have to do any work today."

But the fear-based bridal mags will be sure to let you know that your venue is a reflection of your personality, a testament to your belief system, an unspoken declaration of your priorities, of your spirit, a juicy clue in the case of "Who the hell are Jennifer and Paul, really? Besides co-workers who used to fuck on top of the paper shredder, which is how Paul lost his thumb." Like I always say, it's all horrible and great. There is no such thing as "the perfect venue." Because perfection is a subjective standard that will only bring you disappointment when things are not perfect. And they won't be. Because that's life.

So I'm going to play the role of your bitchiest, most miserable guest and judge all venue options harshly and equally because the truth is, you have to pick what makes you *happy* (that is, *satisfied*).

LOFT SPACE

Hi, are you a funky shared work space?

Hi, do you think you're Andy Warhol and this is your "studio"?

Hi, are you Maggie Gyllenhaal in *Dark Knight* before she got pushed out a window?

BARN

Hi, is your ring bearer Babe: Pig in the City Who Goes Back to the Country?

Hi, is your officiant Mr. Ed's grandson, Ed III?

Hi, is your signature passed appetizer panko-crusted corn nibblets?

SUMMER CAMP

Hi, so I guess this means a lot of your "camp friends" will be there?

Hi, can we stop pretending potato sack races are cool in an ironic way?

Hi, can I please eat in the same lunchroom you ate in the day you discovered masturbation?

INDUSTRIAL MODERN—REFURBISHED FACTORIES

Hi, did this used to be a distillery, 'cuz thanks for reminding me I'm in AA?

Hi, so are we pretending exposed brick still titillates us like it did in '94?

Hi, wow, how innovative, an old broken pipe as a fountain?

BALLROOM

Hi, do you think you're Cinderella?

Hi, do you think your husband is a "prince," because I'm pretty sure he's a data analyst at I-don't-know-where because every time he talks about it, I nod off?

Hi, is this a ballroom or a dank casino that slot machines have been temporarily moved out of?

BACKYARD

Hi, is your chuppah an old swing set?

Hi, did you know your parents' cat just ran across the dance floor?

Hi, we get it you've seen *Father of the Bride* . . . part 1. Part 2 was crazy.

BOTANICAL GARDEN

Hi, if I could name more than five "botanicals," this incredible biodiversity might be meaningful to me?

Hi, I'm freezing. Is it that you were just too cheap to get enough heaters?

Hi, get over yourself. My eyes aren't watering because I'm so happy for you two, they're watering because of pollen?

ANYWHERE IN CENTRAL PARK

Hi, we get it you're Charlotte?

Hi, do you love horses that pull carriages, you animal-abuse apologist?

Hi, the smell of horse poop is threatening the elegance?

ROCK VENUE

Hi, are you hoping your marriage will be the cool marriage?

Hi, the racist graffiti on the bathroom mirror is a classy touch?

Hi, it's so sweet that you're getting married in the exact same spot Henry Rollins once pissed on an audience member?

MEXICAN RESTAURANT

Hi, this sounds perfect . . . because chips?

CHURCH, TEMPLE, OR ANY RELIGION-AFFILIATED SPACE

Hi, way to impose your beliefs on everyone?

Hi, hard to enjoy your vow exchange when a bloody Jesus is giving me side-eye?

Hi, isn't this place a little funeral-y?

Hi, can someone tell the ocean to shut up during the ceremony?

Hi, a seagull just shit during the ring exchange?

Hi, I fucking HATE wind, or as you euphemistically call it, "sea breeze"?

And before I stop being a bitch about venues, a few words on CITY HALL . . . Ever since the end of the *Sex and the City* movie, when Carrie and Big finally tie the knot at city hall, the whole concept of "It's just about you and me . . . and literally nobody else" has been romanticized. It's chic, it's edgy, it's adult, and it's fabulous. Your girlfriends show up with champagne, you're bravely wearing the vintage suit that (*gasp*) didn't cost a fortune, just a (*gasp, gasp!*) small fortune. So humble, so real, it's just about you and Big. Amazing. God, your priorities are so . . . prioritized. But at the same time, do you hate family? Do you hate parties? Are you so up your own ass that you can't bother to give your parents a celebration that honors them? STOP. All of the questioning needs to stop.

Why does going to city hall have to be viewed as outlandish, or sad, or cold and distant, or romanceless, or anything other than what it is? Getting married. It should be an option. Not a frowned-upon option. Just an option. A fair, rational option. You *can* have a party afterwards. You can also *not* have a party afterwards. It is all personal and optional. If your parents still want to throw you a party because they're heartbroken that you didn't have a wedding and they have been setting aside money to pay for it, congrats to them! They successfully save money, which is more than most people can say! The money can go towards something else, like your first house, where their grandchildren will one day live. Grandchildren are more valuable than guac dip and small talk. OR, your parents can take a cruise, just the two of them, because it's about time they say, "Fuck off, kids! Mom and Dad are going to St. Lucia."

Feeling bummed out, but slightly freed? Good.

See, all venues can be shit on. If a venue was supposed to represent your life perfectly, then your ceremony would be held in line at Walgreen's and your reception would take place on a couch.

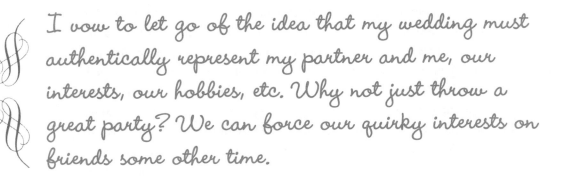

I vow to let go of the idea that my wedding must authentically represent my partner and me, our interests, our hobbies, etc. Why not just throw a great party? We can force our quirky interests on friends some other time.

TRA-DISH
it out!

TRADITIONS ARE A COOL WAY OF TEACHING PEOPLE ABOUT YOUR and your fiancé's respective backgrounds. Like a family tree project in elementary school that's way more loaded than it sounds.

BIG BRIDAL SAYS: **Look through the old scrapbooks. What did Nanny and Pop Pop do? Have you forgotten your heritage completely? Time for religious guilt!**

I SAY: **Smoke 'em if you got 'em, but not all of us have particularly inspiring histories to replicate or riff on!**

My parents got married in my dad's mom's living room with, like, six people present. My mom wore a dress from Strawberry, which is like Forever 21, but with more pleather options. Also, their engagement story as told by my mom is "I was in your grandma's car with your dad. She said, 'When are you guys getting married?' Your dad said, 'In two weeks.' And I was, like, 'Uh, good to know!'" SO romantic. Also, my mom told me that while she and my dad were living together, my dad went out on a date with another girl while my mom just hung at home. What a couple!!!!!! They are still married, though, so I'm not going to question too hard, or I'll just end up in a downward spiral analyzing the source of my daily anxiety.

For me, this is a tough one because my background is Jewish on my mom's side (but nonpracticing, agnostic) and Baptist on my dad's side (also nonpracticing, agnostic). In other words, white as fuck. Dan grew up Jewish, celebrating Jewish holidays, but is ultimately atheist. He just likes the way Jewish traditions bring people together, and I go along with it because agnostic people are "whatever . . ." about everything. Dan wanted us to wear yarmulkes at our wedding and sign a ketubah. I was, like, "What's a *ketubah*? A Jewish tuba? Is someone going to play it?" Point is, his traditions are more tradition-y than mine. Because mine are nonexistent.

My friend Anika's family is from South India, and she found some cool ways to incorporate tradition into her modern New York City wedding. She did a ceremony called *Mangal Pheras*, where she and her husband walked around a grouping of candles on the floor seven times, each time representing another promise to keep in their marriage. It was lovely, minus the fact that every time Anika circled, I thought her elaborate Vera Wang dress was going to catch on fire. It got dangerously close to the flames. All of the bridesmaids gasped in unison seven times. Still a delightful experience, though! And all of the food was delicious South Indian catering, which I panicked over because Dan is a finicky eater—especially when there's no meat for my little meathead. (Said with thickest Andrew Dice Clay–level New York accent:) "This buffet is all chickpeas, no bacon!" But he ended up loving it. "I like the spices. Very flavorful."

Play Fast and Loose with Tradition

When in doubt, if there's a tradition that you're considering, just go for it. It adds interest even if it seems outdated or strange! I think it's because *the older you get, the more you love learning*. When you're a kid, the last thing you want to do is go to a museum, unless it's the Natural History Museum, and even then you spend the whole time wanting to see the blue whale and/or dinosaurs. But as an adult, museums are a legit weekend activity. Reading a book is a fun treat. Scanning a newspaper is a pleasant pastime. All the things you'd rather die than do as a child are fun to you now! So a wedding that has an element of "Hey! America isn't the only place on Earth, even though it thinks it is!" is truly refreshing and educational. Even if it's not your family's tradition. Hell, borrow from a friend's.

I will toss a few rituals into the wedding as I please, and let them mean as much or as little as I desire.

Fuck Hue!

NAVY, GOLD, LIGHT PURPLE, DARK PURPLE, AND . . . CRIMSON?
Wait, what about orange? What about that bright pop of color? No, I can only have five colors. Martha Stewart says only five . . . But I want six! One's gotta go. Who will it be? Orange or red? Orange says "Playful!" But red says "Passionate!" I haven't thought this much about colors since I was learning them in pre-K! This is like Sesame Street *with the emotional intensity of* Sophie's Choice*!*

> **BIG BRIDAL SAYS: This isn't a game. You can fuck up big-time, if you're not careful.**
>
> **I SAY: Choose colors you want, tell the professionals, and see if anyone objects.**

The first question our florist asked was "What are your colors?"
"Um, blush and gold. With white, dark red . . ."
"Lavender goes well with those colors."
This made me as giddy as a tween ordering a glow-in-the-dark retainer post-braces. My favorite flower is a dusky gray-purple rose. But based on Big Bridal, I thought it would be overkill to have five colors in my palate, so I eliminated it, like a joyless goon. I thought two colors was the limit. Maybe three if you're a lamebrain indecisive type!

But now I had a florist—a flower expert, a petal professional, a stem *not-cell* researcher—telling me to break the rules I had put in place because they apparently never truly existed outside of fear-based wedding publications.

So we had our colors. But what next? Are all colors going to carry equal weight, or do we have some colors be the base and others be the accent pieces? I almost lost it again.

Hear me out: Have you ever been drunk at a wedding and noticed the color scheme, let alone seen it as a deal breaker in how you enjoyed the experience? "Mark and Tiffany seem so in love, but poppy red and key-lime? I'm going to load up on the lobster mac at the buffet and enjoy this last hurrah, because after tonight this friendship is dunzo."

The fact is, any color can be deemed a symbol of wealth, or horror, depending on how you associate it. Here's a list of colors to consider in your wedding palate, and a classy association so you feel rich and in charge, no matter how problematic the shade:

"Shit" brown $\longrightarrow$ Louis Vuitton Brown

"Looks like it belongs on a rapper's name plate" gold $\longrightarrow$ Palace of Versailles window trimming gold

"Oh, no, my hair follicles are dying" silver $\longrightarrow$ Mercedes hood ornament silver

Khaki like my high school crush who rejected me wore with his North Face fleece $\longrightarrow$ Gucci tote beige

Bubble gum stuck under a desk $\longrightarrow$ Chanel pink

"Nineteen-seventies couch your mom won't get rid of because it's 'mod' despite a suspicious stain that is either your nephew's throw up or, God forbid, your dad's semen" orange $\longrightarrow$ Hermès Orange

White, like my first baby blanket that burned in a house fire $\longrightarrow$ White like Katie Couric, who is very sophisticated!!!!

Turquoise, the color of my aunt's Arapaho-inspired necklace that she often wears to singles night at her church $\longrightarrow$ Tiffany Blue, because for some reason we see it and go, "Oooooh, diamonds must be nearby!"

INSPIRATION
superhighway

IN THE ART OF DESIGNING THE DECOR OF YOUR WEDDING, A LOT of people will tell you that you need an organizing principle, a wedding decor thesis, a "Story You're Telling"—something to guide your choices. "Start with a pattern you love!" "Umm . . . polka dots?" "Perfect! You could do, like, cute little polka-dot place cards that say, 'Tying the Dot!' Could you die?!" Yeah. I could.

BIG BRIDAL SAYS: You need to find a muse, but don't worry, it can be anything . . . a classic film or a piece of jewelry! Well, not *anything*. Don't use cheap jewelry . . . and if it's a film, please let it be an Audrey Hepburn vehicle. This will help communicate your style ideas to all of your vendors.

I SAY: "An old movie or a broach! Choice is yours!" Are those muses? Aren't those just . . . things you like? Why is it always about Audrey Hepburn with you people? There have to be more films that inspire weddings than just *Breakfast at Tiffany's*.

When Dan and I visited our florist for the first time, she immediately confronted me about my lack of vision, saying, "You sent over a lot of different pictures, so I'm having trouble understanding what you like." I probably confused her further by responding, "I like modern, but I also like antique."

I flipped through her big book of weddings she had done arrangements for, and it quickly became apparent to me that white roses paired with white hydrangeas lent itself to a "fluffy" look, which I'm into because Dennis is fluffy. Plus, I was really struggling to make this outdoor wedding feel as indoor-ballroom as possible, and somehow white flowers have an inherent formality to them. Probably because they're clean and neutral. Again, I am indecisive. I don't want to choose anything. I want it all. So white is a great base for me. I highly recommend it if you are terrified of color like I am. Not terrified of the *look* of it. It's not like every time I see a pink rose I scream, "My corneas! Oh, how they burn!" and fold into the fetal position. I'm just overwhelmed by how to use color, so I avoid it altogether.

But there was one thing that did excite me: Over a year ago, I saw this thing on Pinterest—these mirror trays to put candles on, so the light reflects off of them. That was the ONE thing, out of all the decorations I pinned, that stuck with me. Probably because it didn't seem impossible to obtain. It's essentially just a piece of glass.

Laura the Florist, or "Laurist," showed me some candles that would go on the trays—gold votive candleholders—and I said I also liked more modern vases, to mix and match modern and antique. She showed me a perfectly cylindrical tall vase; I asked what we would use to fill the cylinder, since the flowers will just rest on top. She said she could put LED lights at the bottom. I said, "Can we put some curly willow in the water." Those are those whimsical tree branches that I feel ties in nicely with our fairly whimsical garden venue . . . She said, "Sure."

So there you have it. Our flowers will be mostly white, accents of the other colors I mentioned, antique gold candles to tie in with gold in the color scheme, but plenty of modern vases to confuse everyone into being like, "What time period are we in?"

You're in ALL of the periods, people!

Finding a muse is not essential. It's a lot of pressure, and I truly, madly, deeply (Savage Garden, anyone?) think it can cause you to turn a blind eye to combining different themes, which is way better for I-like-everything-and-nothing people like myself. Knowing what you hate is more important than knowing what you like.

This is what I call the *Anti-Muse*. It's the negative space, which can be just as valuable as the positive space when it comes to aesthetic decision making. Knowing what doesn't light up your brain, motif-wise, style-wise, taste-wise, is a great way to narrow down who you are as a bride. If it gets to the point where you don't really like any decorations—flowers, candles, coconuts spray-painted gold because your theme is "Tiki Chic-y"—feel free to decide against pretty much all of them. Put your money towards amazing music or amazing food or an amazing savings account! Decorations add ambiance, but they do not make or break a party.

I vow to utilize a muse, or five muses, or no muses, and I will call them to my aid as I wish, but I will not make my wedding journey a search for a muse who is my god, whom I fear and worship and make all my vendors fear and worship. I will know my anti-muse—the few or many things I hate, and I will manifest their anti-presence at my wedding.

Wedding Party

(THE INNER CIRCLE)

A CIRCLE SO IMPERFECT,
it's a fucking trapezoid

BY INTRODUCING YOU TO THE CHARACTERS IN MY WEDDING circle, I hope to (a) comfort you by feeling relief these people are not coming to your wedding, and (b) inspire you to take a frank look at the humans you surround yourself with. After all, they are bound to affect the wedding as much as the lighting design or venue.

Before you even begin to think about who will be attending your wedding, it can be helpful to take stock of the people who will be present during the planning. Here are mine:

"Char"

THE STRONG-WILLED JEWISH
MOTHER OF THE GROOM
(CHARLENE BLACK)

- Dresses in 90 percent Lululemon, 10 percent Kirkland Signature from Costco.

- Calls at least once a week to see if I have added knives to my registry. (Is she trying to murder me?)

- Was reportedly told by her boss that she is "too good at her job" and therefore "intimidates co-workers." I feel that this was her spin on "You're a bit much."

- Always needs to "pick something up" at Lord & Taylor. (Is that even a good department store? She is shockingly loyal to it.)

A favorite Charlene moment: When I visited Long Island, I went with Charlene to her workout class she does every Saturday—cardio kickboxing taught by a buff black Adonis named Raymond. Before we went in, Charlene warned me, "The class is exhausting. Most people can't do the whole hour, so feel free to leave early and get a coffee in the cafe downstairs. I'll meet you after." I laughed this off and arrogantly stated, "I have pretty good endurance." She's sixty; I'm thirty. I've got this! Fifteen minutes into high-intensity Hades, I said "Fuck this" and walked my pathetic tired ass to get a blended Matcha with whip, while Charlene continued jabbing and uppercutting to Sia remixes for forty-five more minutes like a true boss.

"Lenny"

THE FATHER OF THE GROOM WITH A PONYTAIL

(LEONARD BLACK)

- Former rocker. He met Charlene because she was a band groupie.
- Has a ponytail and, according to Dan, has always had a ponytail. #PonyDanza #PonyRobbins #MyLittlePony
- Wedding and bar mitzvah photographer on Long Island. (Wants to shoot our wedding, which scares me because the trend in Long Island wedding photography involves color-correcting the grass to be bright green à la *Ghostbusters* slime.)
- Watches any and every show on TV, even the most obscure ones, to the point where he'll be like, "Have you seen that show *Lethal Cheese Slave*? It's on this new subscription network called Thulu, which is like Hulu, but for people with thyroid conditions? Anyway, Selena Gomez is amazing in it." What?

A favorite Lenny moment: Lenny told me he stopped watching *Big Bang Theory* because he didn't like Kaley Cuoco's "new look." To quote him, "The show got bad when she got fat." Interesting deal breaker. For me the deal breaker for that show is . . . that show.

"Dad"

(MARTIN LEE)

- A Southern sweetheart with a closet full of demons.

- Worked as a concert promoter for twenty-five years; is now a schoolteacher.

- Talks about a great art history book he read, but will never open up about his sex, drugs, and rock-n-roll days. Iggy Pop played the music venue my dad used to own. There's no way that wasn't a scandalous cocaine fest.

- Lost 80 percent of his hearing from concerts. Dropped his hearing aid in the driveway and ran it over with his car. Drives my mom crazy.

A favorite Dad moment: When I was in high school, my dad would water our front lawn wearing nothing but a Nirvana hat, V-neck tee, and a jade-green Speedo. In other words, pantless. My matron of honor saw him out there before we became friends, and when we became friends, she said, "I don't know your dad, but I am a huge fan based on his lawn-watering attire."

"Mom"

THE SOCIALLY AWKWARD MOM; MOTHER OF THE BRIDE

(LIVIA LEE)

- Smartest and most creative woman I know.

- Contrarian: Whatever you say, she will disagree—even if later she starts to agree. This comes from the fact that she watches many true crime shows, so her brain is usually in "devil's advocate" mode. She falls asleep to crime shows. She doesn't count sheep; she counts suspects on *Forensic Files*.

- Publicly reprimands my dad for not understanding technology, yet won't check her e-mail and doesn't understand how to delete voicemails.

- Has been to very few weddings and doesn't understand the culture surrounding them—which I love and admire. I had to explain to her what a bridal shower is.

A favorite Mom moment: When my friend asked her bridesmaids to wear red shoes, and I didn't have a lot of money to spend, my mom took me to her favorite secret discount shoe store—a stripper clothing store in a questionable neighborhood in North Dallas. I managed to find a pair for $9.99, and the heels were opaque.

"Moi"

(JAMIE LEE)

- Gullible pushover. (Perfect for Charlene, the assertive overlord.)

- Afraid to speak up for what I want for fear of backlash from in-laws/Dan resenting the fact I have no backbone, or maybe too much backbone? Am I actually . . . stubborn? I don't know what's real anymore.

- Constantly trying to decide on a wedding diet plan that isn't too crash-y, but def low in carbs, but also realizing that diets don't work and are stupid.

- Decided Dan and I should go to couple's counseling to figure out how to create a healthy balance of power between the families during the Wedding Planning Process.

Favorite Jamie moment: Writing this book for you, gorgeous party poodles!

"Dan"

(DANIEL BLACK)

- Funniest person I know.

- One time went to the psych ward because he was worried his hair was falling out, even though he is far from bald (another thing we will be discussing in therapy).

- Excellent dancer. I never knew I found good dancing attractive until I met him.

- Has great taste in clothes. Like, surprisingly excellent. When he likes my outfit, I know it's a great outfit.

- Makes the best sweet potato chips, and always gives me the slightly burned ones because he knows those are my favorite.

- Very close to his parents, speaks to them multiple times a day. I talk to mine, like, once a week—if that.

- Keeps saying "Whatever you want" for the wedding, but really wishes I would defer to his parents' suggestions.

Favorite Dan moment: Dan had to watch a bro-y movie because he was having the actors from the film on his podcast. He called me halfway through, riled up. "It was so misogynistic, I had to turn it off. I can't endorse that kind of ignorance."

"Shebbles"

THE STRIPPER WHISPERER; BEST MAN

(JACOB SHEBTON)

- Intelligent and personable. One of my favorite people in the whole world.

- Was awkward looking when he was younger (according to him) so he is making up for past time by fucking anybody who will fuck him, which is a surprisingly large number of people. He is basically a horny Ursula the Sea Witch from *The Little Mermaid,* only he's offering poor unfortunate souls his penis in exchange for a self-esteem boost.

- He's hooked up with so many strippers that there is a real possibility he will bring one to the wedding, which I'm into. I love body glitter. (He ended up falling in love with a beautiful, hilarious actress named Shauna, and she was his date, happy to report, but sadly there was no glitter.)

Favorite Shebbles moment: Shebbles and I went to dinner when I was visiting New York, and he told me how he was in love with this girl named Shauna who was in his sketch comedy group. I said, "Does she love you back?" He said, "Absolutely not. She has zero interest in me." A month later, she was his girlfriend, and they are still together.

"Bonnie"

THE ONE PROPER GROWN-UP; MATRON OF HONOR

(BONNIE PATTERSON)

- Been friends since age five.

- Effortlessly gorgeous.

- Lives in a suburb of Austin with her husband and two stunning babies.

- She is super calm, kind, and polite. She might take issue with something another bridesmaid does, but will have an unshakable poker face the whole way through.

Favorite Bonnie moment: When we were kids, I was an asshole with a sharing problem. We were making these figurines out of Sculpey clay, and we both decided to make pigs. I gave Bonnie a small amount of pink clay and gave myself a much bigger chunk. Her pig ended up being much cuter because he was tiny, and mine was clunky and burned on one side. This moment defines guiding principles in my life now: Work together. Help each other. Less can always be more.

"Erin"

(ERIN BOYLE)

- Met in physics class in high school. Erin had a crush on our teacher, who had a ponytail that went so far down his back, it grazed the top of his butt. (Second ponytail mention in one chapter.)

- Is a paper guru—makes gorgeous invitations, signs, and all things *papier*. Also dabbles in floral arrangements and made stunning bouquets for my rehearsal-dinner tables using flowers from fucking Trader Joe's.

- Was my rock during the WPP (in addition to the rock on my finger . . .).

Favorite Erin moment: The night before my rehearsal dinner, Erin and I shared a room at Westlake Village Inn and we had a sleepover. We drank wine, watched some shitty movie on the hotel TV that I drunkenly paid twenty-two dollars for, and I obsessed to her about my spray tan fading before the wedding.

"Dennis"

THE '70S BUSH WITH EYES, AKA THE ANIMAL SAINT

- Our furry little chocolate Labradoodle.

Favorite Dennis moment: Every morning when he sits on my head like it's the actual dog bed I bought for him that he never uses.

And those are just the main characters. Even when guest lists are kept small, the process of planning a wedding involves, by its nature, too many cooks.

CHERISHING, AKA HANDLING,
your wedding circle

TREATING YOUR WEDDING CIRCLE WELL CAN BE THERAPEUTIC, especially if you make it fun for you. But fights may happen, too, and it's okay.

> **BIG BRIDAL SAYS:** Throw your partner's mom a bone by letting her make some choices . . . She'll feel useful and like you.
>
> **I SAY:** Maybe read a book on codependence, send her a copy, too, and face up to her now.

Do you want to spend the rest of your life handling disagreements in this fashion? Now is the time to show *Bother*-in-Law who you are, and what your limits are. This doesn't mean don't hear her out or silently fester for months and then suddenly snap at her when she asks what topping you want on your froyo. "Cookie crumbles, goddammit!" It does mean not letting yourself get bullied. One time, Dan's mom called up yelling about how we needed to invite kids to the wedding, and as soon as I got on the phone and said, "Yelling like that isn't going to work for our marriage," she backed down and we had a rational, mature discussion. It was a small, but significant victory. Also, saying the phrase "our marriage" is actually quite powerful. It's like a force field shielding you and your partner from emotional toxicity. Use it!

Another tactic? Practice less contact with the family. You don't have to update them every second—even though they might want that. Dan's family loved status reports because talking about the wedding felt like part of the fun, and a lot of times it was helpful because saying out loud what I needed to get done was an instrumental first step in actually doing the damn thing. There were other times where, if someone asked, "When are save-the-dates going out?" I would, in my mind, punch a wall and let the blood from my knuckles coat the floor like mop liquid. Here's the thing: You are not obligated to give status reports—it doesn't make you bad or ungrateful; it makes you an adult. You're allowed to be an adult with adult needs even though your wedding makes you regress into a child again—asking parents for money, listening to them tell you how to live your life, asking for their validation. You are not a child anymore. Remember that.

Speaking of keeping the inner circle happy while simultaneously clocking them out of planning or stressing you out: Presents for parents and MoH and co-MoH are an awesome antidote. I really enjoyed giving back to the people who helped this whole thing come together. I went to a pottery painting place in LA, Dan and Dennis tagged along and hung out, and I painted jewelry boxes for my mom and Charlene and put notes in them. Then I did these mugs for Bonnie and Erin. It was more selfish than anything because I straight up LOVE ceramics. Gimme a bowl, and I will glaze the fuck out of it. Plus, zoning out on a creative task was good for my overloaded brain. I was able to decompress while doling out gratitude. In my twisted head, a giant coffee mug is a legit great gift. Coffee is a top priority for me, and oftentimes mugs are not as large as I'd like them to be. The one on the bottom of the next page was the size of a toddler's head.

YOU'VE GOT IT maids

ANYTHING GOES WITH HOW YOU APPROACH THE BRIDESMAID tradition these days, but it's nonetheless Dramapalooza. It feels like some high school nonsense we are forced to navigate as adults. Like deciding whom to share a limo with to prom.

> BIG BRIDAL SAYS: **Figure out what's important to you in a bridesmaid. Make a rubric and ruthlessly use that criteria to say yay or nay! They'll be so honored you asked.**
>
> I SAY: **Asking someone to be a bridesmaid is like asking, "Hey, would you like to pay to ruin our friendship?" The responsibilities can be overwhelming and, depending on the bride, not worth it, especially if she ends up mad at you, or worse, "not mad, just disappointed."**

I started by making a list. These are the people I know I would want . . . the A list. Then we get into the B list. How fucked up is this??? I don't like that I even just said or thought "B list." But let's face it, there is a B list. And the reasoning behind the B-versus-A list is interesting. It doesn't have to do with closeness or even liking this person more than that person . . . It has a lot to do with AVOIDING DRAMA. I just know that certain people, while I would love to ask them to be in my *till-death* squad, will bring a great number of issues to the situation.

One friend, for example, is the sweetest, and we get along so well. Like family, we can argue and be fine two secs later. She is refreshing in that way . . . BUT she has a meltdown about her life practically every week. She won't even call me crying—that would be great, actually. She just sends me about twelve texts in under five minutes, and the last one is always, "I could really use a friend right now where are u?????" It's a LOT.

Then there is the friend I like. We have fun together, but she is genuinely annoying. She has commonly held opinions, but she declares them like they're shocking revelations: "I'm the type of person who believes women should be paid as much as men."

No matter whom you choose, I hate the term "bridesmaid" because it implies that you are some kind of czar and they are to wipe up after you when you shit on the floor. I know that is not the actual expected responsibility, but there is a dark shadow attached to the term "bridesmaid."

First of all, it lets the people in your life passive-aggressively know where they stand. Which I hate. Because I never walk around actively going, "Jane is my favorite, followed by Jill, and Karen is a close third." I don't rank my friends. Some of my friends I've known longer than others; there is a bond from just years of being in the trenches together. And some of them I hang out with on occasion but don't necessarily enjoy, which is bizarre and horrible. I spend time with them because we mesh well enough to get a pedicure together every other month or see a YA teen-living-with-cancer movie together because if I asked Dan to see that, he would throw himself off a rocky New England cliff. But there isn't that *Beaches* closeness of "Wow, she is the Bette Midler to my Barbara Hershey! I would let her daughter bring her cat to live with me!" feeling to our relationship. Nah, we're not that close. And I didn't even fully face this icky truth until

I got engaged. Because getting married suddenly forces you to see where everyone stands in your life. Your wedding becomes a deadline. "Dissect and evaluate your friendships by *this* date." Barf. I would rather be in the dark like before.

Choosing bridesmaids can also force you to confront the current status of your oldest friendships. As I mentioned earlier, I felt distant from one of my best friends/bridesmaids, which sucked. Having pal drama as an adult, not a hormonal middle schooler, is more stressful than Kirk Cameron's career path. Whatever the nuances of your friend feud, I encourage you: Communicate with the people you love. You will have the thing where you call and pray to Yeezus it goes to voicemail, then they pick up, then your voice gets shaky, and you have some shallow conversation up top before digging into the shit-bucket of unfortunate feelings. "How was that charity pie-eating contest? Loved the pics on Facebook. Anyway . . . I DON'T EVEN KNOW YOU ANYMORE." But in the end, clearing the air during your WPP is better than pushing feelings down the way a guy "subtly" pushes your head down when he wants a blowjob, but you're all, "No thanks, I'd rather choke on a Twizzler."

Maybe opt for no maids? Why not?

I'll tell you why not: Because the idea of making your amazing friends a part of your wedding is a huge chunk of what makes it so amazing. The marrying part is fun too, sure, sure, sure. But just getting to hang with all of your favorite people at one time? How often does that happen? And asking them to be a bridesmaid is a great way to ensure that they won't bail! Because they can't! Because you've trapped them into being by your side no matter how inconvenient it is for them. Yaaaaay!! Deeming someone a "bridesmaid" is the same thing as booking them, like a venue or a band. If you want them, you have to reserve them ASAP. Think of yourself as a talent agent and your friend as your client. You are getting them a gig! Your wedding! Only instead of making them money, you will drain them. But, hey, you never said you were a GOOD agent!

That said, I had been stirring about asking people to be my bridesmaids because as much as I love the idea of saying "Hey, I love you, please be with me on my special day," I also feel like I am inconveniencing them. The implication is that they have to spend money on me, which makes me uncomfortable. Even if I did it for them. So I tried to find ways to make everything super cheap for everyone. It was hard.

Don't fret over those who don't make the cut. It's nice to let people off the bridesmaid hook. And you don't have to go giving them some other task to make them feel useful. They're not children! You can still spend time with them during important moments. If you want to invite them over to the bridal suite while you're getting ready, do that. Include them like you would in any friendship hang.

My friend Carrie invited herself over to my suite the morning of my wedding, and I was thrilled. There seems to be this misconception that if you aren't in the bridal party, you aren't a beloved and dear joy in the bride's life, and that's very untrue. I had considered asking her and another friend to be a bridesmaid but ended up thinking it would be easier to have fewer bridesmaids . . . it had nothing to do with how much I value them.

When Carrie arrived, I jumped up with only one eye made up, the other completely bare, like bridal *Clockwork Orange*, and we walked to get coffee from the hotel cafe while bridesmaids were starting on their makeup. We had a fun little chat on the way over about how I wanted her to hook up with Dan's friend. In fact, it was one of my favorite moments of the day. I appreciated that she didn't give too much power to the title of bridesmaid—because that's all it is. A title.

HOW TO KEEP YOUR BRIDESMAIDS HAPPY:

- Shower them with gifts, even if they are little gifts. I bought these little heart-shaped boxes from Michael's and decorated them, put their initials on them, with glitter and stuff, and filled them with confetti and a little note that says "I love you! Be my bridesmaid?" Not a *gift* gift in the true sense (they can't swipe it for a Starbucks cake pop), but I tried to set the tone that I care and that this won't be a miserable experience and I am sorry that they have to spend money on me because, generally, I hate that.

- Be understanding—someone can't make it to your bachelorette? You are going to be too drunk to remember they are there anyway.

- Be mindful of people's financial situations. The first e-mail you send to your group of bridesmaids about your bachelorette should say something like, "The cost is $250 per night, per person to stay at The Cosmopolitan. Does that work? Please let me know." Not, "It's $250 per night. Please Venmo me or send me a check to the following address. K. Bye." Always ask first, and try to make adjustments where you can, so everyone can come.

HOW TO KEEP YOURSELF HAPPY WITH YOUR BRIDESMAIDS:

- Lower your expectations of them. In general, this means fewer upsets during the process.

- Do something shitty to them. Not insanely shitty, but mildly shitty—like make plans and then cancel them last minute. That way, when they are shitty to you later on in the WPP, you can be, like, "Eh, this is karma," versus feeling blindsided by a letdown.

- Have them send you a list of their top five weaknesses, and you send them the same list. That way, when Jenna is being irritable because she ran out of her go-to stash of Swedish fish, you'll better process why she just called your four-year-old nephew a douche wagon. "It just slipped out." "No worries, boo. You need your fix, and he was rummaging through your purse."

- Pretend your friends are characters in the movie that is your life. If everyone was a good guy, flawless (i.e., boring), you wouldn't have a compelling movie. But if one is the anti-hero, one is the hot-mess alcoholic, one is the divorcée who is trying to get laid even though she has her two sons with her . . . etc. It all becomes a great story versus an unfortunate amalgamation of unfortunate personalities.

- To quote the brilliant and hilarious self-help author Jen Sincero, "There will never be another you. You're kind of a big deal." Unfortunately, books are published to be consumed by the masses, not just YOU, the one and only YOU, but all of the YOUs, plural. Each person in your life is a YOU, so you do you, and let them do them! *Their* you and *your* you will not always align. It's a two-way street. But it's what makes the world rich, complex, goofy, stupid, and beautiful.

- Send out a manifesto with a purpose of intent. E-mail all of your bridesmaids letting them know the kind of bride you hope to be, the kind of bride you fear you will become, the kinds of things that you care about (e.g., centerpieces and cake?), things you don't care about (dinner *shminner,* get up and dance, people!), and, even if it's tough, what you look for in bridesmaids. Do this as soon as you've trapped them into doing it so they aren't rear-ended with any psycho behavior from you.

- Bungee jump. It will replace all thoughts of "Shirley hasn't responded to any of my e-mails about bridesmaids' shoes" with "Fuckfuckfuckfuck." You'll be so focused on not dying that you won't even entertain thoughts of friendship minutia!

Assigned Bridesmaids Dress vs. "Wear What You Want"

I was in the "wear what you want" camp for so long. Every bridesmaid dress I've ever worn, I hated, with the exception of one because the criteria was "Everyone pick a gold dress." And all the girls had great taste and similar shades of gold, so it just worked. I ordered that dress on Rent the Runway for thirty bucks. It was awesome.

When I was asked to be a bridesmaid in my best friend's wedding, and I saw the dress she picked out, I remember thinking the seashell that crept up over my boobs made me look like I was being eaten by a giant taffeta clam (see right). Also, yes, I cropped out my ex-boyfriend.

But here's the thing about taffeta clam: Bitch looks good in photos. And when everyone has the same dress, it is ONE LESS THING TO WORRY ABOUT. Nobody has to send you pictures for your approval, with captions like, "Is this the right shade of beige pink? It feels more pink than beige, is that okay? It's more *Peige* than *Bink*."

I remember a girl I used to work with telling me that her bridesmaids just picked black dresses and that was the uniform. If you like black, do this. It truly is the easiest solution. But if you're like me—a frantic Pinterester—studying photos of bridesmaids lined up on either side of the bride—you know that shot?—you'll notice a few things:

- Black is drab.

- Black does come in different shades.

- Some girls might go short; some might go long. Consider determining a standardized length.

- Shit, black really is drab.

There are certain trade-offs between price, color, and sizes when it comes to bridesmaid dresses. When I wanted everyone to wear different shades of gold and blush, I went on various sites—Nordstrom, David's Bridal, Saks—and they were all super expensive. Rent the Runway was cheaper, but my bridesmaids are not American Girl dolls with the same body type, different heads. Two out of seven were pregnant, and some of the designers on RTR offered a limited range of sizes. Plus, length is an issue. You can't hem a dress you are renting, so there's the chance of your bridesmaid wearing an alluring Carolina Herrera gown . . . and tripping on it, like Dopey from *Snow White*, but way hotter.

Azazie.com is the way to go. I do not have a deal with them, I do not make money by saying this. It is just true. They have hundreds of colors, hundreds of styles, every size, and the fabric is nice. Also you can have everyone pick a different style, but in the same color, so there's variety that way, if you want variety.

I really think everyone wearing the same thing is just a safe bet. For your sanity and for theirs.

HERE ARE WAYS FOR EVERYONE TO FEEL
"PERSONALIZED" VS., LIKE, ONE GIANT
COMMUNIST YOU-SERVING UNIT:

- **Jewelry.** Buy different earrings for everyone. Gift opportunity! And they actually will wear these again.

- **Hair.** Let them choose their own style and have fun with it. One of my bridesmaids rocked a sleek high-n-tight Kim K pone, while another girl went with a crown of braids, Renaissance Fair–style. I was hoping she would walk around the wedding eating a giant turkey leg and greeting guests with a Cockney accent to complete the vibe, but it didn't happen. #HugeLetdown

- **Makeup.** Let them take control of their own faces, for heaven's sakes. Don't micromanage other people's lids and lips.

- **Shoes.** If their dresses are long, maybe everyone wears black, nude, silver, or gold shoes. Something they already own. Send out an e-mail, see what people have in their closets, and go from there.

Guests

(THE OUTER CIRCLE)

YOUR WEDDING
dot biz

WEDDING WEBSITES ARE VAGUELY EMBARRASSING. WHAT, IS YOUR marriage a business with nothing to sell but people's belief in your love? However, they are helpful to people who don't have space on their fridge for save-the-date magnets or a Filofax to store your information cards.

BIG BRIDAL SAYS: **Make it reflect you and your fiancé!**

I SAY: **Make sure it is a one-stop shop for everyone attending the wedding. Also, it doesn't have to match your reception theme. At all.**

For anyone hesitating to make a website, it's not hard. Don't go asking a "tech-y friend." Sites that help you make wedding sites are designed for people who don't make websites, so let this be your opportunity to realize that the Internet was built for you, too.

Try for the easiest-to-remember domain name possible, and optimize it for mobile (you can just click a button that says "optimize for mobile"), because a lot of people will be going to this website when they're running late because their girlfriend's curling wand in fact *wasn't* plugged in and heating up the whole time she was doing her makeup, and they need quick info about where they need to be and when.

Feel free to load up the home page with the key details for people looking stuff up in a pinch. Anytime anyone asks you a question that's annoying via e-mail, upload it (with or without their name) under FAQ, thus preventing a similar e-mail.

Write up some BS about you as a couple, if you're into the idea of you being part couple/part brand. Some would argue that a wedding is a Brand Launch party . . . a fund-raiser for a new startup (please drop cash in the vintage birdcage!), so if it delights you to wax obnoxious about who "we" are . . . then go for it. But consider that people might quote it at you for the rest of your lives. "Ben knew Valerie was the one when they both fell asleep at the same John Mayer concert, and were startled awake by Val's guttural snoring."

I tried to recap my proposal for the "About" section of our wedding website, but it was a surprisingly tedious feat, recalling the order in which each moment occurred to create the most accurate representation of the event. It was like writing an IKEA manual. "How did he ask?" felt more like "How to assemble an ASKHOLMEN (outdoor table set)." There's very little excitement in just writing out a blow-by-blow of a situation, no matter how significant it was.

You can keep it simple and just describe the story of how you met. It does not have to describe your proposal in detail. Just a few paragraphs that clue everybody in and make them (and you?) excited to be a part of this love fest.

Here's what my "About" section said:

It's how all great romances begin: They met as guests on a podcast . . .

Dan and Jamie met in LA in 2010, when neither of them even lived there. Jamie just finished working on *Ridiculousness* and was planning on heading back to New York soon. Dan was in town performing his hour-long UCB show *Sit Down and Shut Up NYPD Variety Hour.* Their mutual friend, Rob Stern, who was also in *Sit Down,* decided to tape a special LA edition of his podcast before heading back to NY.

As guests, Rob had on Jamie as herself, but Dan came on in character. So when Jamie first met Dan, he wasn't even Dan. He was Donny Domingo: an abrasive Italian gentleman selling a product called Protein Roids. (Not a far cry from who he is out of character.)

Jamie thought "Donny" was one of the funniest people she had ever met, and was wondering how they were both in New York doing comedy, but had never met until they were randomly in LA? Weird.

When Jamie returned to New York, Dan came to see one of her stand-up shows. After her set, Jamie sat down next to Dan and said, "We should hang out sometime!"

And hang out they did. The following week they saw each other every night, meeting up after shows or at McManus, the UCB NY hangout bar. When Jamie had to go out of town, they would text nonstop. It was s'cute.

On their first official date, Jamie took Dan to one of her favorite New York restaurants, Momofuku Ramen Bar, where

Dan stressed out over the menu. Too exotic. No chicken parm options. Dinner was also on the shorter side because Dan needed to watch an MMA fight that started at 9:00 p.m.

It was love at first bloody headlock.

After two years of living together in Manhattan, Jamie and Dan decided to move to LA, for more space, more jobs, and more avocado.

Today, they live in Los Feliz with their newest little family member: Dennis the Labradoodle.

Important: Put this fun cutesy stuff in a separate section from hard-nosed facts. People don't want to skim through ". . . And right as he took a knee, a jogger ran by and screamed, 'Are you getting engaged?!'" when they're late to the reception and need that address fast! (BTW, that did happen during Dan's proposal.)

Inevitably, people will text you anyway, so create a chunk of text with links, and put it in your notepad on your phone, so whenever friends and family text you with questions, you can copy and paste that block and shoot it over to them.

- **Airport information.** What are the first, second, third closest airports, if your wedding is not in a big city.

- **Restaurants and activities in the area, for out-of-town guests.** I guarantee nobody will take any of your recommendations, but it feels like a nice gesture. If they need to know where to eat, if there's even time to eat outside of eating at the wedding, they'll use Yelp. "But my wedding is in Jamaica! People will want to explore!" No, they'll want to sit by the pool, imbibing caloric coladas and judging people's bikini bods through their sunglasses.

- **Registry.** People will ask you where you are registered, and you can just direct them to the website rather than giving them the spiel. "Crate & Barrel, Bloomingdale's, Target, Honeyfund." "I went on the Crate & Barrel site, but I didn't see you on there." "We're on there." "Weird. I'll try again while I'm on the phone with you. One sec. My computer is slow to load." YOU'RE SLOW TO LOAD! KILL ME!

TRANSPARENCY ABOUT WHO IS SINGLE

One thing wedding websites are missing is a transparency about who is single and ready to . . . fuck. (Oops, I'm bad at rhyming.) It's a real bummer that there isn't more time in the Wedding Planning Process to just straight-up focus on who is available and which friend of yours you could pair them with. Let them know about a system you'll be putting in place.

- Single people get a different color cup to drink from the whole night.

- An after-after party will take place for people who just need to get a BIT more drunk to make a move.

- Ready to Minglers are seated in a fenced-off area. Guests can bet on who will hook up. Bonus: Post odds on a decorative placard.

GUEST LIST *gauntlet*

CREATING A GUEST LIST COULD BE AN EXASPERATING JOB, BUT you can get through it. Many have done so before you. That is a comfort.

> **BIG BRIDAL SAYS:** Figure out your guest list early because it affects everything. If you double your guest list, you'll need to adjust all meals to half portions to stay within budget.
>
> **I SAY:** Why are you a cruel taskmaster? If I double the list, I could just serve one entree per table, and leave a jug of whey protein and a few blendie bottles there for nutrients.

You have to invite your friends and family, and for some reason your parents will want to invite friends of theirs that you don't really know. There's already the groom's family that you don't know and probably some of your own extended family that you don't really know, and now you've got your dad's old Dungeons & Dragons buddy from college talking your ear off about a Lady Larping League in case you're interested in joining.

Beyond just considering the number of guests, the types of people you invite also influence other choices. If you cut all your old PETA buds off the list, you probably don't need as many vegan options floating around. Invite them, and you'll probably opt against the white fox-fur-lined veil.

Guest Quest

Guest lists can become a real fiasco, and there is no clean way to get through it. Perhaps, try this decidedly tortuous but less painful path through figuring out whom to invite.

- After grabbing your digital, analog, or other method of name jotting, start with the Shoulds. There are probably some people you feel you "should" invite. Some Definites. The Shoulds are the toughies, and a place where you'll want to focus your chopping efforts up top. Think Family. Friends of parents. Other Shoulds from other seemingly essential aspects of your life. List those people now, and if *no one is coming to mind,* use some kind of clever search of your e-mail inbox to remember all the people you supposedly cherish. Facebook probably has some answers if you can't remember your childhood friends and whom you're related to. If your parents are alive, they will likely add plenty of their compadres to this list for you. Parents tend to think of children as pets, and thus when their pets do something interesting, it's something they want to show their friends. Also, you'll get a bunch of Shoulds from your partner—their parents probably know a bunch of fools. Jot a note about those for now as "That List of Other Shoulds"—having that there will remind you as you work on your list that you can't really control whom they invite, only the total number. This might inspire you to be better at chopping. Since you don't know them, and it will be harder to argue over their importance individually, to reduce the likelihood of these randos attending, you'll have to cut down your own to set an example of guest frugality.

- Feeling overwhelmed and annoyed yet? Good! That's how you know you're really doing it.

- Pause to consider a radical option. Just send out a single message saying, "If you think you belong at my wedding, like you're pretty sure, then shoot me an e-mail. Why should I have to chase you down?" It's like when teachers allow students to "grade themselves." Then you can debate people directly if they think they belong and you disagree. Hopefully, enough people's self-doubt will kick in, and they will be too shy to state their desire to attend. These lovely humble types you can always circle back to and give them the invite they deserve. Yes, the meek shall inherit.

- Okay, if you don't go radical, and you need another pick-me-up after looking at all the Shoulds, take a moment to list ten people in your life you just truly love and enjoy (all these numbers are based on averages—and you can scale up or down as needed), people whom you deep down would just love to have join you at this special event!

- Now look back at the Shoulds, and allow yourself to feel your resentment if it exists. Then look through the Shoulds, and pluck out the ones who happen to be Shoulds but also happen to be someone you value (maybe that's grandma). Pull these technical Shoulds (but actually "True Blues") over into the "Lovelies" list of ten. They don't deserve to be over there in Should Land. It's not your cousin's fault that she happens to be someone you'd invite no matter whether you liked her or not. Now you should have left an isolated list of True Shoulds—where Shouldness is their only real reason for being on the list. If your own father is still stuck in Should, then it's time to ask some tough questions.

- Now let's further narrow down True Shoulds based on the type of Should at play.

  a. Identify the people you feel you *should* invite because *they* will be pissed and bitch about being snubbed, even though you believe they have no right to be. Consider whether you want to continue to perpetuate their deluded ideas about your relationship and life in general. Maybe it's too much of a headache to destroy their worldview with one non-invite, which could cause serious blowback while you're trying to plan the event. Read up on codependency and decide what you value. You can't be held hostage by other people's emotions. Maybe this is a swift and convenient way to let folks know where you stand, which can be, much like giving someone their weekend back, yet another gift.

  b. Flag the people who are giving you an active bad feeling. Maybe there are some people from your past you're suddenly in the mood to confront. Perhaps do that now (six months or further out from the wedding), and if they handle it well, give them an invite.

  c. People from your partner's list. This is not really within your control . . . so check in with who is paying . . . if it's them, then, well, this is one moment where you have the right to decide to send back all the money and use whatever you have in Amazon missing-package credits to plan a wedding . . . without having to be beholden to anyone else's wishes. Think that through, and then make your choice.

- Having done an initial trimming of your Shoulds, it's time to set aside that dungeon of souls and head back to the Lovelies, whom you're excited about—this is your ten you just love, plus the people you love whom you brought over from Shoulds. Focus on them, feel the love, and then start to expand from that place of warmth. Write or speech-to-text the names of all the people you'd love to have at your wedding, if your wedding was free, and anyone could attend.

- Utilize Facebook to keep from forgetting someone. Yes, there are people not on Facebook, but at least, if you forget them, they won't see the wedding photo album.

- E-mail your closest friends and say, "Who would u expect to be at my wedding." Sometimes other friends are better at remembering who your friends are.

- Search through your e-mail, with keyword phrases like "I miss you" or "It's been forever." That's a quick way to draw up some friends you may not have seen in a while.

- Once you have too big a list, then you can start cutting, but don't skip the too-big-a-list part, or you risk forgetting someone. Marvel at how expensive this would be. Ask yourself whether you are Cinderella and have the prince's fortunes to celebrate with the entire kingdom.

- Steel yourself to let go of feeling bad about not inviting people! Remember, not being invited to a wedding, for most people, is a relief. Don't think of it as a snub. You're giving the gift of freedom for a weekend. Even if the pictures of the good time hit their Instagram feed, the uninvited will have a sense of calm because they didn't have to find something to wear, buy a present, or get a hotel room to hang out with people they were friends with five years ago. Those are classic Cuspers . . . the college friends you lost touch with because you're not going to hang out with them if they don't live down the hall from you. You wouldn't have really hung out with them then, but they always had their dorm room door open and would stop you when you were walking by. And now he's dancing to "Shout" alongside your Holocaust survivor great uncle? Seems unnecessary.

- Once the guilt is gone, it's time to come up with a chopping method, whether to julienne fools off the list using "How long it's been since you last wore said item, I mean, hung with said person," or push 'em to the edge of the table and let 'em fall in the trash, metaphorically meaning, to say that "No one who makes me feel bad about myself attends!" Whatever seemingly cruel or deeply healing criteria you develop, remember that you're not "cutting" anyone, you're "setting them free."

- Consider sending those you'd rather not invite a little card with a "one weekend to do as you wish" voucher . . . suggesting that while you like them, you value them enough not to ask them to come to your wedding but instead to spend it however they want!

This kind of back-and-forth zigzagging journey might seem crazy, but crazy is normal in this process. So embracing it is really your only option.

Not a list person?

Okay, so in case you skipped the last page because working on a guest list still feels too nerve-racking, first of all, that's okay. Second, there are other ways. Consider clearing a wall or finding a blank one (in your artless home) and writing each name on a Post-it note and sticking it on the wall. Instead of crossing people out, you can move them around, from "yes" to "maybe" to "no," pretty easily.

One thing I noticed post-wedding is that some people didn't get an invite simply because I forgot about them. If they had been there, would I have been psyched? Yes. One friend asked how my wedding was, and I felt the need to say "Oh! You should have come!" but there's no real way to say "I completely forgot you existed for a minute." You have to just own your lapse in memory and play it off like it was an intentional deliberate choice you made to leave them off the guest list. That, in its own horrible way, is less offensive than "I forgot you were a person in my life."

Another complexity that can come up: you hooked up with your fiancé's friend before you knew your fiancé, and your fiancé doesn't know and wants to invite him. This happened to me. Luckily, the guy wasn't able to come to the wedding, but if he had been there, we would have just done the dance of avoidance. Ain't no thing.

Even more complicated: the ex-boyfriend who was your first love, whom you are still on great terms with, and who can't get an invite simply because it would be too weird for you and for him. This also happened to me. In fact, when I first got engaged, my excitement was coupled with panic about "How am I going to tell my ex? Will I invite him? Will he attend?" The answers are "No, I won't," and "No, he won't." I am friends with his sister, so she got an invite and he didn't. So uncomfortable. But it was just the way it had to be. I thought about not inviting her, but that's awkward. "You share genes with your brother, sorrrrryyyyy." Check your guilt at the door when it comes to shaping your guest list. Tricky decisions have to be made, but your gut will ultimately craft the list into being the way it should be to maximize the fun you have at your wedding.

I vow to navigate my guest list in any way I please, and to alter it whenever I want.

PRETTY MURDERED TREE CORPSES,
i.e., invitations

THEY FEEL LIKE A BIG DEAL BECAUSE THEY GO TO PEOPLE'S homes, a pretty little treasure buried deep in their rubber-banded clump of bank statements and J.Jill catalogs, and while I'll try to steer you away from using them, let's assume you are, and discuss the issues.

> **BIG BRIDAL SAYS:** First impressions . . . you only get one. An invitation is the "first impression" your wedding makes, so it better reflect all aspects of what's ahead.
>
> **I SAY:** Oh yeah right, like if someone shows up in a decidedly vertically oriented, rough linen, scripty mood, they just won't be able to have a good time at a slick, modern typeface, sharp, cardstocky event.

Since it's recommended you send out invites at least three months in advance (save-the-dates anywhere from six to nine months in advance), and you'd therefore need to order those invites months before that, the expectation that your invite matches your wedding requires you to really nail the vibe of your wedding way up front. That's stressful. How can you get around that kind of pressure?

- Make your invitations a total postmodern freak show of style. Lace edges and calligraphy with satin embellishments, a wasteful amount of plastic, and all sent inside an envelope that's actually plantable. Plant this invitation and watch a tomato plant sprout!

- Aim to say absolutely nothing with your invitation. Go so simple and mysterious, but not in a way that seems to betray any ambiance. Think: Size 11 Arial font on crisp white paper. Like the business cards in *American Psycho*.

- Cut out letters from a magazine and make your invitation look like a ransom note. They'll be, like, "Are Don and Heidi alive?! Guess you'll have to attend the wedding to find out!"

- Realize that most people are gonna wear what they're gonna wear based on their own style and vanity and body concerns, not based on your invitation. Regarding the dress code, keep in mind that most people are incapable of creating a different look for a Luau Wedding than for a Black Tie. My invitation said "Black Tie Optional" and one girl at my wedding wore a dress that looked like a figure skater's leotard. It was up-to-her-butt short with lots of skin-colored fabric with rhinestones stuck to it, glittery and naked: like Tinker Bell, if she was trying to seduce Peter. She really clung to that "Optional" directive. If you're concerned that everyone you know will dress and act according to your invitation's style, then send a bunch of different kinds of invitations—that way there will be a variety of styles showing up. And you're free to do what you want. They'll look like the crazy kooks, not you.

Invitations are optional, really, and a Paperless Post, Appy Couple, or the like, is totally fine. An online invite is easily linkable to an online calendar. It's more likely the info gets transferred from a website than from a heavy invite that keeps falling off your fridge. I'd also like to point out that my ninety-four-year-old grandfather has two e-mail accounts and checks them daily. The misconception that "Elderly people can't handle technology" has got to stop.

Once you are at peace with the above options (and they really are options), when you think about going back in another direction, maintain a sense of perspective. Maybe you don't need three different textures. Or maybe you do. Maybe your heart soars when you flip through samples in a binder in the back of Papyrus. If the romance of the USPS holds nostalgia for you, then go for it. You're allowed to go crazy on invite costs, and then serve Doritos at the wedding.

There is a lot of pressure around hand addressing stuff—if you do buy into this, consider at least letting go of the idea that you have to master an old-world calligraphy style. If you are thinking about hiring a calligrapher, not to judge, but you might be a bit of a whackjob. Hire one if you want. No biggie. But at least consider allowing the charm of your chicken scratch to trigger memories in old friends of letters you sent them from camp or prison.

Keep in mind . . . there is a real expectation of sending thank-you notes after the wedding, so you still have another opportunity to practice penmanship by a window, pretending to be a Brontë sister, ahead of you. The allure of hand lettering might wear off before the invites are done, and you'll have no delight in those thank-you notes.

- Look for a stationer (that is a real term) if you're interested in sitting at a table and flipping through binders. Otherwise, embrace the Internet. None of the samples is stained or fingerprinted online. Embrace the Internet whenever something doesn't sound like THAT much fun to do in person. Ignore friends who claim to "basically be stationers" because they've made their own greeting cards before—it's not clear if they're capable of scaling their services, and don't let your wedding be their learn-on-the-job experiment. Or do. Maybe your entire wedding could be a growth experience for amateurs looking to go professional. If everyone from stationer to chef to dress designer is semi-pro, that might create a nice underlying theme that will subtly tie all the parts together by a vague sense of shittiness.

- When you meet with a stationer, try to annoy them by calling them a Stationiere (like Lumiere, the spunky candlestick from *Beauty and the Beast*) or a Stationeuse like Chanteuse. It's always good to start off on a disrespectful foot. They will then try to shame you by throwing terms at you, like "copperplate" and "sans serif" and even "slab serif." Luckily, it's not your job to know those terms. You are not a stationer. (Unless you, ya know, *are*.) You just say, "Let me see the samples." You're the queen, baby! Okay, you're at least the customer, and you can point and have fun refusing to learn their terms.

- You will be asked about what you want written on the invitation, so this might be a good time to finally ask spouse-to-be whether they're willing to admit their true full name, etc. *What is Riky really short for? If it was short for Richard, it seems like you'd spell it Ricky.* Do a double check on spelling of spouse's parents' names—don't trust your own spouse about how to spell their parents' names. They might simply not yet have nailed that down in life.

Then, there's the idiotic démodé wording on wedding invitations. "Mr. and Mrs. Martin Presnell Lee request the honor of your presence at the marriage of their daughter . . ." It's clunky, it's pretentious, and I've always had a personal distaste for the mother of the bride's name being swallowed whole by the father of the bride's name. I'm also an advocate for both sets of parents being represented on the invitation because putting the focus on the bride being "given away" by her father feels like she's a sofa on a sidewalk.

Initially, I wanted my invites to say "With their families, Jamie Lee and Dan Black invite you . . ." Then, it was more specific. "The Lees and the Blacks invite you to join in honoring the marriage of their children Jamie Lee and Dan Black . . ." Then Charlene said she wanted her name included, so it landed at "Livia & Martin Lee and Charlene & Lenny Black invite you to . . ." I made sure the moms' names went first. It felt like my own little middle finger to the tradition of the FOTBs getting all the glory.

Info to include on the save-the-dates, which should go out five months before the wedding if you are like me (again, like, eight months prior if you are not):

- You and your partner's names.
- Wedding date.
- Wedding city (Venue info can wait at this stage, if you want).
- Wedding website (Optional. Can wait til the invite, I say!).
- That's it!

Info to include on the invitation, which should go out three (eh, two is fine) months before the wedding:

- All of the above, plus . . .
- The address of the venue.
- Your hashtag.
- RSVP card with pre-addressed and stamped envelope.

- A note that says, "For more info, visit our wedding website." Otherwise you end up with a bunch of tiny cards that your guest is now expected to keep track of. A meal card, an RSVP, a "details card" (my matron of honor used this term around me and I punched myself in the uterus). So many cards, too many! Can you include the meal choice on the RSVP? Does it have to be separate? Why do invitation envelopes have to be more cluttered than a hoarder house of cats? Consolidate, consolidate, consolidate.

For the "RSVP by" date: This is where you get to be selfish. You should have people reply by a date that (a) makes planning a seating chart easy for you, and (b) fulfills your caterer's needs because they will need a final head count likely one or two weeks before the wedding.

Here's the hard truth, the cold hard facts of life, peeps: A lot of guests won't give AF about your RSVP date. They'll just put that little card in the mail whenever they feel like it. Or they'll never mail it back. They will just tell you they are coming when you see them at, like, a birthday party that they didn't even know you were going to be at. "You're friends with Ted? He's kind of a dick. Was that TMI? I'm wasted. Rachel and I broke up, and I'm taking it pretty hard. Anyway, I'll be at your wedding. I don't have the RSVP with me, but can you just, like, mark it down in your phone or something? See you April third." "The wedding is April thirtieth." "Right. The thirtieth. I fucking miss Rachel . . ."

No Kid'n

AWKWARDNESS WITH POTENTIAL GUESTS CAN OCCUR WHEN their lives and lifestyles clash with your desires for your wedding. How you choose to handle this likely depends on your confrontation style.

> BIG BRIDAL SAYS: **If you are having a kids-free wedding, just come up with a cute phrase that starts with "We love your kids but . . ." and hope people won't complain.**
>
> I SAY: **If you dance around the fact that you don't want kids, it leaves the topic way too open for discussion. Own your choice and say, "I don't want kids there, because I don't want kids there."**

People know how kids act and the tone they set. No matter the formality of the event, a child will have stains on his face and shirt, cruncha-munching on animal crackers. (Not even a fancy cracker . . . couldn't you go Club for the evening? Or those super crunchy ones with the seeds and nuts that are stale on purpose? Until your saliva rehydrates them? Just-add-water crackers? I dunno what they're called, but they go great with goat cheese.) One couple put "2½ attending" on their invitation reply to me, referring to the woman, her husband . . . and the baby. I wrote what I thought was a polite e-mail, blaming everything on myself, "Oh, I must not have communicated effectively." Here's what I wrote:

"Got your reply, so glad you're coming! Unfortunately, we are doing a no-kids wedding. I am so sorry I didn't make it clear on the invitation, and I promise we aren't heartless assholes. Hope this doesn't throw a huge wrench in your plans. Please let me know if I can help in any way. Xoxoxox"

The couple's response? "Cool. Count us out then."

This e-mail made the blood drain out of my face, like I had seen a ghost, or a fat-free donut. Something horrifying. Yes, it sucks that you have to find a sitter, but it would suck way more to have the harsh cries of a finicky newborn drown out someone else's "I dos." Also, this couple got married two years before me, so you'd think, when you've been a bride yourself, you'd have sympathy/empathy for other brides. I might be a raging dillweed for saying no kids, I'll wear that label, I'll have it stitched onto my shirt like the Lacoste alligator, but being a "bitchy bride" really just means owning your opinions and sticking to your guns.

My sister-in-law Emily insisted on having her sons, ages two and four, there, and I caved because she was part of the inner circle. There was a moment when they ran across the dance floor in their footsie pajamas— she had *promptly* changed them after the ceremony. How dare you wear your Old Navy sleepwear anywhere *near* my Monique Lhuillier, five-grand, Chantilly-lace gown?! I wanted to punt the little shits up and away between the string lights. Field goal! Ultimately, I was very glad I did not have (any other) kids at my wedding. I stick by this decision and still feel strongly that my nephews should have gone to bed before the reception.

REGISTRY, AKA KICKSTARTERS for materialism

IF I HAD TO FILE A PREFERENCE ON GIFTS, IT WOULD BE TO drop a check in the box at the wedding. That's fun because the day after the wedding we get to total the amount and deposit it in our account. It's like I'm a landlord and EVERYONE owes me rent. In a perfect world there would be no need for a registry because all your guests wrote you a sweet check. Unfortunately, there are some cheapskates who want to get you a gift to sort of mask that they only spent $32 on you. There are also the narcissists who want you to think of them every time you make fondue. People need to be given options because, if there is any barrier between them and buying the gift, they will go rogue, and you'll end up the proud owner of two dozen soda streams.

BIG BRIDAL SAYS: Take inventory before registering.

I SAY: I agree. Somehow I've ended up with nine, count them, *nine*, sauté pans because I just registered all willy-nilly.

In theory, wedding gifts used to be the way a town came together to help a couple create a new home, but these days a lot of people are shacked up already and don't need all that crap . . . But they still want stuff because anytime there's a tradition that has ever included gifts, you feel like you're getting shafted if you don't clean up. Back when couples needed to be outfitted with basics by the community, a registry allowed guests to pick things to the couple's taste and not overlap gifts. Cool.

That's all fallen away . . . except for the entitlement to gifts. Yes, some people are still using it to start or round out a collection of Le Creuset (even the pepper mills and kettles, which are not made of the famed enameled iron!), but now that you can register for anything online via a multitude of glorified Amazon Gift Lists, couples just ask for stuff they want: canoes, forty hours with a personal aerial acrobatics trainer, jars of basil pesto.

You may be tempted to start a Honeyfund, the insufferably cute term for helping a couple go on that add-on "horses on a beach trot" during their honeymoon. The idea is "We don't want to make you buy us china, because we don't use china, so we don't want to waste your money, but we do *want* your money . . . just send us on a trip and buy us dinner; also, we'd love to see *Hamilton*—orchestra please, our eyesight is failing prematurely, and if it's not orchestra seating, are you even really seeing the show?"

Here are my hot tips for . . .

The Earlier the Better. While normally, I don't like to push the Earlier-the-Better agenda of Big Bridal because that feels like an attempt to extend your time in the Big Bridal store as long as possible, there is a benefit to others in getting stuff up early, as soon as people receive a save-the-date. Why? Because cash flow isn't what it was in the '80s. Sometimes people have enough credit on the card to buy you a gift today, an entire year before the wedding, and they'd rather do it now than wait, and possibly end up empty-handed.

Variety Is the Spice Rack of Registries. The benefit of having a variety of types of items on your registry is that it's more fun for your guests. Not everyone gets joy out of subsidizing eight more spoons in your spoon collection. Guests scroll through your list, yes, looking for stuff within their price range, but they also look for something they don't think is totally stupid. Give your Wiccan friend an opportunity to buy you a cauldron—it will make them so happy.

The Stories Your Registry Tells. Feel free to be aspirational, but keep it believable. When guests are scrolling through your registry list, they can't help but conjure a scene in their heads as a result of your list—high balls, a bar cart, crystal swizzle sticks, and a Draper table runner. We get it. You have visions of you and your partner turning into late '60s *Mad Men* party-throwers the second you're married. That may be true, but keep in mind some guests might be more willing to buy you beer mugs based on the style of your last "party." Keep it real. Also, watch out when putting healthy versus less healthy food cooking items on the registry. Judgmental mofos might try to steer you towards health—if you put up a pizza stone and an ice cream maker, and your self-righteous Pilates-obsessed aunt insists on buying the Vitamix . . . you might be like, "Of course you didn't buy anything carb-related, you tyrant," which is kind of a rude thought to have when someone spends $300 on you.

Two Stores No Longer Means Walking the Mall. Register at two places that are national chains:

1. A cheap discount store like Target for your cousin who just got out of rehab and whoever else at the wedding who will be trying to put a positive spin on their "Why I moved back into my childhood bedroom" story. Have everything you pick from there be around $40. If you run out of things to get, register for Melamine dishware, a stack of cocktail napkins, and some fancy toothpicks. Side note: Try to sit all the unemployed guests at the same table so there isn't a lot of investment or vacation-home talk during which they have to pretend to get a text message.

2. The other store should be at the nice end of the mall, which isn't an issue online, but don't make it too fancy. You don't want to look like an out-of-touch brat. Bloomingdale's is great because it's not elite like Barney's, but it's also not depressingly utilitarian like Sears. Load up on expensive stuff there. Nothing under $150. That way you might get some people to write checks, and those who don't will be punished.

Celebrate the Nongifters. No matter how easy it is for people to order from your registry, some sociopath will ignore your wishes completely and get you some Lennox garbage they found on a clearance table in the "gifts-from-assholes" section. Or, worse, one of those decorations from Home Goods that's like a wooden sign with HOME SWEET HOME "painted" on it. The person who gives no gift is way more honest than the sign-gifter. A nongifter is saying, "It's your special day, but I don't really care"; the sign-gifter is calling you an idiot. They want you to believe that you just received a handcrafted piece of woodworking from a dear, toothless old man in a small Southern town, when clearly it was highly mass-produced. If you get one of those, be sure to alert the police because that sign-gifter is probably a nefarious sociopath.

JUDGY WUDGY
was a guest

NO MATTER HOW MUCH THOUGHT GOES INTO YOUR FLORAL arrangements, creative cuisine, abundance of food throughout the night, ease with which guests can get to the bar, how perfect the temperature in the room is . . . people are talking shit behind your back. I know this because I've done it at every wedding, and likely so have you. And if you haven't, you hold things in and that's not healthy. Check yourself.

> **BIG BRIDAL SAYS:** Make your wedding so perfect that everyone will be delighted and impressed and love you more than they already do.
>
> **I SAY:** Nah. Everyone will talk shit about you.

The shit-talking varies from wedding to wedding, obviously. Some weddings it is a minimal throwaway complaint: "I wish they had passed more feta canapés. Oh, well, dinner is soon. I can deal." Other weddings it's more intense aggravation: "They're only playing swing music? I want to dance, not feel like I'm in that Nazi movie with Christian Bale that I can't think of its name!" (*Swing Kids*!) Other weddings it's straight-up petty hate: "The bride's hair looks ridic. She looks like trailer park Medusa with all those tendrils coming out of her head. Tendrils are just curls who thought they needed to lose weight but went way too far."

Point is, shit will be said behind your back. "But I worked so hard to make everything perfect!" Doesn't matter. In some way, you failed in the eyes of a guest or guests. A wedding is a high-stakes event, and that is in direct proportion to how much people will *talk* about it.

In fact, let's take a proper moment together to let that sink in. Repeat the following phrase ten times in the mirror (crying optional): PEOPLE WILL TALK SHIT ABOUT ME AND MY WEDDING, NO MATTER WHAT I DO TO PREVENT IT.

Think of it as a calming affirmation. It's so sad, it's actually great.

REASONS FOR SHIT-TALKING:

- **Jealousy.** Your guest is jealous. Of you, of your relationship, of a scarf you found at T.J. Maxx that they'd kill for? Who knows! No matter what you do, she will find fault in your wedding. And yes, I said *she*. Because guys don't hate weddings the way girls do. Is that sexist? Probably.

- **Their man thinks you're hot.** He said it to her only once and he claims he was kidding, but she can't get over it. And at your wedding, you look more radiant than ever. So she will be shit-talking you all night, mostly because she's miffed her Rent the Runway dress is ill-fitting. Her date says he thinks she looks great, but she knows it gathers at the hips. She feels upstaged by you. Hence the shit-talking!

- **They're getting divorced.** They are currently deciding who gets to keep the Pottery Barn wine rack, the West Elm party platter, oh, and their children. And now they have to watch you prance around in a white gown, showing off your perfectly contoured face and temporarily thin wedding body. It's just a lot.

- **They hate their job.** Or they don't have one right now. I once went to a wedding when I was very unemployed and literally all I could think about was how expensive gas would be for the car trip from LA to San Luis Obispo, and how the friend whose couch I was crashing on had a cat with an oozing eye infection, and would the ooze get on me when the cat slept on my head? "If I somehow caught the cat's infection, how much would it cost to see a doctor? I don't have health insurance." Oh, and the friend whose wedding I "sacrificed" for got divorced less than a year later.

- **Friend-sion tension.** You and your guest are not on great terms. You invited them because you've known them a long time, or they used to be in your inner circle, but there was a fight or general weirdness that neither of you resolved. I say: Resolve it before the wedding. Tie up those loose emotional ends before the big day if you can. If you feel too stressed with planning, I can assure you that the stress is exacerbated by the fact that you are also at odds with a pal. If you choose to address it post-wedding, be warned that if they make a rude comment about your bridesmaids' dresses, your food, or your band—even if they don't exclusively play swing music—it's probably just that their anger from unresolved issues is spilling over onto your poor innocent "cute-iful" wedding.

- **You actually messed up.** You tried to save money by having a taco bar instead of a full three-course dinner. But taco bar to the caterers just meant lettuce, cheese, and beans, and they ran out of beans. People are hangry. Get that MoH of yours to order buckets upon buckets of chicken on her credit card stat. Or be *okay* with people not dancing because all they can think about is shimmying their way to Taco Bell as soon as the party is over, while ripping you a new one behind your back.

- **Gossip is fun.** My mom and I connect with each other over negativity. If anything is "off" about a wedding I attend, the two of us will delight in discussing it at length. That is one of the ways we bond. Talking shit is our friendship glue. It's friendship glue for a lot of people.

- Leave funny comment cards on the table. Something to the effect of "We know this wedding isn't for everyone. What could we have done differently? We want the next one to be even better!" A joke about shit-talking and divorce! Killin' it!

- Make one of your wedding details intentionally ridiculous, borderline insane, to satisfy people's Shit-Talk Tooth. The way you give a dog a bone. Give your guests something to chew on, complaint-wise. Example: KidPrint as a menu font. They'll whisper behind your back all night about that one so hard that they won't even notice you spilled wine on your tits.

- Have a confessional booth where guests can go to vent about your wedding. Hire a priest to sit in it (or just a guy named Dave who needs some extra cash until his meditation app takes off), and let the bitchin' begin! Call it the "Bitch Box." Catchy!

- **Your wedding is not home.** People would rather be in bed. Maybe not in bed, but near their bed, on a couch, watching documentaries, Pinteresting holiday side dishes because over the age of twenty-five, people get sleepy—or at least lazy—after, like, 8:00 P.M. I know this because I *am* this. I was worried I'd be tired at my own wedding and want to peace out early. "Do I have to stay for the last dance? Ugh, can't my husband just dance with a stunt double?" Placate these Yawn Heads with an extra piece of cake and let 'em sit the night away while you dance the night away. Bye, Felicia! Wait. Felicia doesn't sound granny enough. Bye, Gretchen!

The shit-talking that occurs at your wedding could come from one of these sources, or it could be a combo of all of them or some of them. But you know what? It doesn't matter! Everybody talks shit at weddings, sometimes before, sometimes during, always after. It is disrespectful and immature and unkind, yes. But talking shit when you are a guest is a relief, a release . . . a verbal orgasm . . . a *vergasm.* Let your guests have multiple vergasms as long as they do it out of earshot of you and your husband. And your parents. And anyone else who is on Team You.

Vendors and Supporting Cast

WEDDING "planners"

"WEDDING PLANNER" SOUNDS DOPE IF YOU PICTURE A GUARDIAN angel swooping in to save the day, and nightmarish when you picture Martin Short in *Father of the Bride* . . . although the daughter in that film did seem to love him. It's hard starting a new relationship with someone during this time, but might they save you stress?

> BIG BRIDAL SAYS: **Wedding planners are a godsend for the bride who is overwhelmed but still wants a spectacular event.**
>
> I SAY: **They can't save you and they aren't superhuman.**

Can you handle planning your own wedding? Of course you *can*. If you have a year, with time management and remembering to trust yourself—your tastes, your instincts—you can plan the wedding, no matter how busy you are. If you have less than a year, you can also manage that. I'm not saying it won't be tough, but I'm saying you can have a job *and* plan a wedding.

"But I'm REALLY busy." So am I. I travel a lot, work for myself, have random deadlines popping up left and right for writing and stand-up and a bunch of other bullshit. I am also not a naturally organized person. I lose my sunglasses every day of my life. As I write this I currently have no idea where my car key is. It's just one key, not even on a ring. I need to get a ring. You see the point I am making. But hear this and hear it now: *Having a wedding planner does not mean you won't be busy with wedding planning.*

I am not here to pigeon poop all over the idea of hiring a planner. Do it! I wanted a wedding planner from the beginning of this whole process—because it felt glamorous. Celebrities have wedding planners! I want to feel like Sofia Vergara when she was marrying that studly Italian Magic Miker! Also, when I initially got engaged, I slipped into the Big Bridal paradigm of "It's all just so overwhelming! What's my color scheme? What do I want my wedding to say about me? Oh me oh my!" I had drunk the Big Bridal Kool-Aid, and it had made me White Dress Wasted.

I held off but I ultimately did it, a month before our wedding. As we got closer to the wedding, I just wanted someone to keep tabs on me, keep me in line, make sure I wasn't forgetting anything. It was nice to have a paid professional looped in, looking out for mistakes and oversights. But Dan and I booked all the vendors, spoke to the caterer, everything fell on us still—even with a planner. Our wedding planner was more of an e-mail forwarder. It was a lot of "See below from the florist," "See below from the band," and "See below from . . . you?" "Sorry, Dennis stepped on my laptop and fired off *ahdn,m585959cno&*pwiu*. I believe that's Doganese for 'Sup?'"

Consider a wedding planner if you fit in one of the following categories: You have a really demanding job, you have high aspirations for your wedding that are going to take a lot to pull off, you're planning a destination wedding, or you simply prefer professional help. Personally, I think a therapist is the most valuable professional help you can have during the

Wedding Planning Process. But back to the topic at hand: I don't think wedding planners are that helpful.

- If you can afford it, why not?
- It makes you feel like you're having the full experience. She may not be J. Lo, but she will make you feel like you're in that movie, which was not a great of a movie, but a lighthearted romp nonetheless.
- You can start sentences with "My wedding planner says . . ."
- He or she can have uncomfortable conversations for you, depending on how personal the situation is.

They should be called Wedding Elves because they are not the omniscient Santa they claim to be. They are not on top of everything. They are on top of *some* things . . . the most obvious things that honestly a ferret could nail if he was rewarded with enough mushed banana and oats. "Planner" sounds way more authoritative than they actually are. They really just recommend vendors they have relationships with, and they keep you on track during the event . . . And I mean the four- to six-hour event itself, not a moment before.

On my wedding day, I assumed my planner would greet me in my hotel room bright and early, warmly embrace me, and say something like, "Are you ready, you blushing bride, you?" Then she would pull a bottle of champagne and flutes out of a tiny purse. "How did you fit all of that in there? It's like a magic trick!" "That's because I'm the Mary Poppins of planning!" After we cheers'd, she would say, "I'll leave you to getting ready, but text me and I'll come right back if you need anything at all. Food, coffee, a chair massage. Whatever you need." Instead, she didn't call me all day. She didn't drop by unannounced to tell me I'm the most jaw-dropping beauty she's ever encountered and she's been doing this for fifteen years so that's saying a lot. I eventually texted her, asking, "Do you have the iPod for the pre-ceremony music?" She wrote back, "No. Please make sure someone drops off the iPod. And make sure they bring an auxiliary cord." What the so many fucks?

So, yeah, reality did not meet fantasy. In an ideal world, though, here's the wedding planner's job description:

- Reading the bride's mind about whom to invite. Assembling a color-coded Excel spreadsheet to illustrate an A list, B list, C list, and C-U-Later list based on said mind reading.

- Sending out save-the-dates to this list. Designing them (she has a brain scanning app that analyzes the bride's personal taste), stuffing envelopes, collecting addresses. They've got this. All you have to do is pose for the engagement photo that is then printed onto the magnets or whatever.

- Mediating conflict. They are in the room for every fight you have with your fiancé, and they always side with you.

- Sending out e-mails on behalf of the bride about: dresses, bachelorette party, bridal shower, rehearsal dinner.

- Handling the rehearsal dinner. Handle this the same way you would the wedding (in short, HANDLE).

- Blocking out hotel rooms. You do it, lady. Call the hotel, get in a fight with Susan in Group Sales about the lower online price not matching the price she is quoting. Honor the online price, Susan. Don't be gross. We are spending thousands at your hotel.

- Booking the honeymoon. You can use a travel agent, but just tell me you are taking care of it. "Where do you want to go?" Uh, reference the brain scan. That's YOUR job.

- Having sex with my fiancé. I haven't wanted to, much, after the mom-overstepping stuff. I actually whisper-yelled at Dan in the baking aisle at Gelson's, "Why don't you just fuck your mom? You honor her more than your own soon-to-be wife." I am a hideous evil beast.

- Walking our dog. He has hit this new phase where he has so much energy. We take him to the park, he runs, he pants, four minutes after being home and napping, he is ready to go again. Can you please help us? I'm trying to write a book.

- Making plans with my friends. Keeping track of whom I haven't seen in a while and either setting up a dinner, or at the very least firing off a "Miss you! Let's get dinner soon" text.

- Washing my face for me. Nothing burdens me more than getting ready for bed. I hate taking off my makeup with a towelette, then cleansing, then wiping my face, then applying Argan Oil. Then I have to brush my teeth, too? And take out my contacts? So many steps I might as well bake a fucking quiche.

NEW NAMES FOR WEDDING PLANNERS

- Plan Drescher
- Jackie Plan
- Plan Weddinghood
- Plannette Benning
- Planna Karenina

VENDOR *bender*

UNLESS YOU GET MARRIED AT A RESTAURANT, AND THEY TAKE care of everything (actually a really good option), you're going to have to deal with different folks pedaling different things you may or may not need . . . aka vendors.

> **BIG BRIDAL SAYS:** Get everything in writing, because being able to point to an e-mail is so much easier than "You said you would do such and such . . ."
>
> **I SAY:** I could NOT agree harder and more-er.

Because my father-in-law is in the wedding business, everyone wants to "give us a great deal." However, when I go to ask what that entails, I get a lot of "Uh, we're working on the numbers now, but don't worry, we'll definitely get you a better price than you would get anywhere else." This makes me furious, and my mom said to me early on in this process, it doesn't matter if you are dealing with a friend, get the deal in writing. It protects both parties. I don't know why I couldn't think to tell myself this, but again, we turn into children during the WPP. "My mommy says . . ."

That's right. I don't have my own adult brain right now. I am renting Livia Lee's.

When my wedding was in New York, before the coastal switcheroo, my father-in-law, Lenny, insisted I meet his favorite florist on Long Island, his buddy Rupert. I said, "Sure thing!" and jumped online to check out the man's website . . . Big mistake. It was so shoddy—a rotation of photos that you couldn't click on to individually scrutinize. They just kept rotating, like a new Mazda at a car show. Plus, the interface was comprised of fugly fonts, colors, and clip art, and to make matters worse, his e-mail address was registered at EarthLink.net.

Competitive professionals don't use EarthLink. EarthLink is for sweet retired moms over seventy who want to forward Panda Sneeze to their kids twelve years late. Lenny said to me, "Rupert is so talented, he doesn't need a good website. His work speaks for itself. Plus, he'll give us an amazing deal. He's my friend." A week later, Rupert and I met at Starbucks on Fifty-Seventh Street. For a solid half hour, we talked about how he had a stint put in his heart, because there was no way for me to change the subject to flowers without seeming like a callous douche. "Yeah, yeah, yeah, your vital organ has a thing in it to keep you alive. I got it. Now, let's talk PEONIES!"

After the meeting, Rupert was supposed to send me a proposal. He did not. I called and texted. No response. He ghosted me. Finally, my mom called from a different number, and he answered. "It's going to be around twelve grand." So the "great deal" wasn't even a concrete number, on a tangible piece of paper, like he had guaranteed after the stint-chat. It was just a verbal ballpark of a giant, exorbitant amount that was way out of my budget. I knew then and there, this was not my guy.

Moral of the story: Don't feel like you are being "too businesslike" with vendors. There is no such thing. And anyone who doesn't adhere to this—even if they are family—is not someone you want to work with. The flipside is you don't get things in writing, and then you later have a tense, cumbersome conversation with the vendor explaining how they've let you down. And legally, they will owe you nothing. You'll be furious, start drinking, pass out in a ditch, and wake up to rats eating your hair.

Vendor Questions and Beware Ofs

Here's my biggest piece of advice: Pick vendors who have worked the venue before or have a relationship with your venue. Not someone you saw on Pinterest you "just have to have." Any vendor is capable of fulfilling your creative vision, because the wedding industry is competitive—everyone has to compete by offering what everyone else is offering. You want the well-oiled machine of a relationship, who works with your venue or wedding planner consistently, not some clueless whac-a-mole who shows up forty-five minutes late because he "doesn't know the area" and your wedding planner can't even reach him because he has a flip phone and Sprint.

- **Caterer.** Caterers will sneakily upsell you while acting like the upgrade costs nothing. Our caterer casually invited us to their showroom like they were inviting us over for wine and a game of Cards Against Humanity and did a mock-up of what our tables would look like. They said, "And we can change the linens on the table if you prefer satin or something with texture over plain white." I was, like, "Yes, please! I love texture!" This was something I've never said before and will never say again. Turns out, swapping out the linens would cost an extra $75 per table. They didn't tell us this when we were at the showroom. They sent us a printout so as to avoid confrontation, haggling, or my inquisitive "Da fuq?" look.

- **Music.** Indoors, most stuff sounds good, but if your venue is outdoors, ask:

  - How many parties have you played outdoors?

  - What equipment do you need or have to make an outdoor party sound as good as an indoor party?

  - Then write down their answer and bring it to your friend who is either a stagehand or in a band to see if they approve. If you don't have this friend, make this friend. Our band sounded like a gaggle of turkeys being defeathered alive because we just assumed they had the right microphones, mixing board, and miscellaneous gadgetry.

- **Flowers.** Even if you are recommended to a florist whom your venue works with, and you get there and the displays in their showroom are super underwhelming, as are the ones you see in their elusive Binder of Best Work, worry not! Fresh flowers are gorgeous—period. If they are a professional florist, who has done wedding after wedding, allow yourself to trust them. (Rupert had worked our venue in New York, but the venue recommended different florists. Very interesting . . .) They know their shit, and if you send them pictures of what you like and don't like, and/or describe your vision—even if it's just "I want it to feel magical!" or some bullshit—they'll do a good job. The flowers do the heavy lifting, not the florist.

- **Videography.** Ask one question. "Will my reception feel like *Attack of the Drones*?" See page 246 for reasons behind this.

Ceremony

PLENTY OFFICIANTS
in the sea

IT'S ANYONE'S GUESS THESE DAYS WHO WILL BE OFFICIATING A wedding. A lot of people opt for a friend. Others enlist a religious type the family trusts. Anything goes, which of course, widens your options and thus gives you another thing to contemplate.

> BIG BRIDAL SAYS: **If your friend officiates your ceremony, it will be much more personal!**
>
> I SAY: **And if a random rabbi marries you because you're getting married on Passover, and you don't have a go-to rabbi in California, make sure you trust them and that they get to know you so they can make it feel personal.**

Dan and I took our rabbi out for Thai food as a last-ditch effort at bonding, because in our previous meetings we hadn't gelled. One major strike against her had nothing to do with her script for the ceremony. She kept commenting on how good Dan looks, how muscular, and said nothing about how I look. Granted, I had only lost three pounds, and Dan had lost fifteen, but that's beside the point! I was, like, "I've lost weight, too!"

She goes, "You don't need to lose weight." I was, like, "Awwwwwwww, thanks." Then she goes, "Tone up, maybe." Bite me, Janice.

She also kept saying, "Dan, I want to come see one of your shows!" And she did. She and her wife went to see Dan do improv, further winning him over and making me feel like the lowly sidepiece. *Bridepiece.* (Oooh, new term for when you don't feel like the main attraction, and you should because you're the bride!) Point is, she connected with my husband more than me.

In these meetings she also always mentioned she's a performer, sings at cabarets, which is awesome! But not once did she ask how we met, where we are from, etc. And those kinds of questions, and the answers they prompt, are what personalize a ceremony.

During one meeting she busted out into a solo on the patio of Coffee Bean. I thought she had a nice (enough) voice. There's something about being at a chain coffee shop, on the patio, among wind-burned dudes with thumb rings trying to write screenplays on clunky Dell laptops, and "earthy" girls wearing paisley patchwork maxi dresses yet aggressively chain smoking, pairing that with the sound of a heartfelt Hebrew ceremonial ballad . . . It was just too much kooky SoCal for me.

Flash forward to the wedding. Before the rehearsal dinner we were supposed to sign our ketubah, but the rabbi was running late. She got lost, apparently, between the Eden Gardens venue and Westlake Village Inn, which is crazy because (a) they're fifteen minutes apart, and (b) we all have GPS! Either on our phones or, for tech laggards, a straight-up Garmin on the dash! Unless my wedding was in the middle of the Amazon, and there was no cell reception, only toucans and yucca plants, there's no excuse.

So the dinner had already started, and I was insanely anxious, waiting for her in the hotel boardroom with our witnesses and various family. I was, like, "Can we do this later???" while Dan's whole family seemed totally fine with missing the $6K dinner we paid for because of, like, God?

I said fuck it and went to dinner. Ten minutes into saying hellos and hugging and excitement, Dan's brother approaches me, frantic.

"The rabbi is here, let's do this quick." I slip outside of the dinner room onto this veranda overlooking the lake. It was picturesque, but I didn't care. *Let me go back to my party,* I was screaming from the inside. The rabbi sits down . . . fiddles to find a pen, fiddles to find the right page to read to us from . . . Come on, lady!!! Even my aunt who is the most religious Jew of us all was, like, "This is irritating." The rabbi could see that I was eager to leave and after I signed said, "Go back to the party." I said "Great!" and leaped up and headed back. But I could tell Dan was annoyed that I didn't take it more seriously. (He should have been annoyed by the rabbi lacking basic human skills such as GPS and having a pen.)

All that said, a quirky trainwreck of an officiant can add a lot of charm and character to your wedding. In the end, our rabbi was another piece of the "Don't take this too seriously" puzzle. She grounded me. With her singing off-key, rummaging through papers because she lost her place, getting out of breath throughout her time at the altar . . . It was so bad, it was amazing.

Here's the thing, though. If you can't have a sense of humor about your ceremony, (a) get an officiant who knows you well, or (b) write your own vows so no matter what happens with the officiant, you end up feeling connected through your words to your partner and your partner's words to you.

I vow to take Adderall before the ceremony so I don't rudely zone out like Jamie did at hers.

RING & FLOWER
people & animals

PERHAPS SOME PEOPLE ARE BRAVE ENOUGH TO HAVE CHILDREN at their wedding, even going so far as to include them in the actual ceremony. This is terrifying to me, obviously. I wouldn't say children don't have their place at the wedding. But I wouldn't *not* say it. Having a dog participate is also a mess, but at least if a dog screws up, you only blame yourself—not the parents. It's a smaller pool of resentment.

> BIG BRIDAL SAYS: **Making a cherished niece or nephew a flower girl or ring bearer is a lovely gesture, and is sure to get lots of "awwwwws."**

> I SAY: **Flower girls and their ilk have been getting too much attention for too long, and you shouldn't be afraid to diminish their role in your wedding.**

I wanted my wedding to be an enchanted evening. In a botanical garden, dancing beneath strings of tea lights, my poofy-at-the-bottom dress sweeping the dance floor like a French lace Zamboni . . . or a five-thousand-dollar feather duster. It's tough to achieve the vibe of decadence and elegance when, before everyone even sits down for dinner, before seven o'clock, Dan's two nephews, ages four and two, have already been changed into footsie pajamas and are running around, eating Goldfish crackers that are crumbling all over the dance floor like they're on an overnight flight to Paris, and their parents are just trying to placate, placate, placate so they don't start screaming and wake up the other passengers . . . Now my dress is literally sweeping up bright orange cracker debris.

Everyone who makes the wedding "cute" also doesn't give a fuck about you or your wedding. Their main function in being at the wedding is to send the message of "I don't hate kids!" If children *have* to come to the wedding, have a designated "kids' area"—if the venue has room and you have money to hire a few babysitters.

Did it ruin my wedding to have children there? No, but I did notice. My philosophy is that no one thing can ruin a wedding, but this did bother me. I think what bothered me the most is that my family-in-law did not let me choose whether I wanted to have kids there or not. They heard me say that I would prefer to not have kids there. Next thing I knew, my sister-in-law was sending me pictures of the boys wearing tiny tuxedos, and my mother-in-law kept saying, "Jason and Max are so excited! They keep saying, 'We want to go to California!'" That's because Dan's family kept saying, "We're going to California!" And they would mimic it back because that's what children ages four and under do. They barely know what a wedding is. Hell, they barely know my name.

Thankfully, I was not obligated to have a flower girl. All she does is throw rose petals half-assed-ly, literally wherever she wants, and everyone sings her praises for the rest of the evening? She twirls on the dance floor, taking the focus off of the bride, or goes skipping across it when people are eating like it's her own personal ice rink. Uh, it's my day, tiny princess.

I suppose it's not the flower girls I'm annoyed with and more the fact that single groomsmen have an easy get-laid gimmick and single bridesmaids are left with nothing. Have you noticed how the flower girl inevitably ends up dancing with a groomsman, standing on his feet, making him look like some kind of good-with-children dreamboat? Suddenly he becomes the guy every single girl wants to sleep with. If you have a bunch of single groomsmen who are aware of this principle, then that little flower girl becomes the most sought-after dance partner of the night.

Single girls deserve a get-laid gimmick of their own, but there doesn't yet exist something as foolproof. If a bridesmaid lets the ring bearer stand on her feet, no guys are going to be like, "Ooh, I wanna get me some of that! She looks like future wife material. Yummmm!" So, I've devised some tricks for gals rolling solo (and yes, it is highly inappropriate to put this in the section on children, but it's my book).

GET-LAID GIMMICKS FOR SINGLE GIRLS AT THE WEDDING:

- Spill something on your dress, near the neckline. Cleaning it off will draw attention to your breasts. (Extra points: Try to get someone else to spill something on you, so you don't come off too drunk.)

- Slow dance with another bridesmaid. This will put the image of a three-way in his head.

- Make a toast where you talk about the time you and the bride went to spring break in Key West and go into graphic detail about the wet T-shirt contest you were in . . . But then round it out to how the bride had been a great influence on you, pulling you off the stage right as you were hosing yourself off. The bride becomes the hero in the story, and you reveal your wild, spontaneous nature.

- Eat cake sexily. Focus on frosting. There's not a lot you can do with actual cake, no matter how light and moist.

- Dance with the grandpa, to show that you *might* be into older men. This will make a potential catch feel boyish in comparison, and then he'll feel the need to prove he has the genuine classic American masculinity of a WWII vet.

- Fake a choking OR fainting next to the hot groomsman so he will feel obligated to save you. Do not be ashamed. You're not being a damsel in distress; you're a woman with a goal who knows what will work when time is limited.

Dogs in Cummerbunds: How to Make an Animal into a Ring Bearer

Everyone assumed Dan's nephews were shoo-ins for the ring-bearer jobs . . . but I was tempted to use Dennis. Kids will drop the pillow, act shy, and forget that they are there for a reason and run off to their mom, cowering behind her leg like it's some kind of protective shield. Dennis would just cut the shit and walk forward down an aisle, as long as there were zero decorations for him to sniff along the way. Of course, this was a wedding-related decision, so I had to think it through.

PROS OF AN ANIMAL RING BEARER:

- They make spiritual traditions cuter. Yes, if every male is wearing a yarmulke at your wedding, the dog should not be excused. You don't want male guests resenting the dog for not having to flatten his hair.

- You get to assign the job of "ring bearer *walker*" to someone who wants to help but isn't in the wedding party.

- Lil' nieces and nephews snubbed for the flower girl/ring bearer job can be disinvited from the wedding! Or serve as bacon wavers, there to lure your Shmoof towards the bride and groom.

- It says, "We're fun, aren't we??" in case there were any doubts, or in case later things get serious due to a hora injury.

- Annoying friends will probably judge your pet's performance harshly, telling themselves that their dog, cat, or iguana would have done a better job if they were called to action.

- Dog cummerbunds are expensive, and they only wear them once!

- Walking down the aisle, the dog could pee on someone's thick leg, thinking it was a tree, or offend a woman in her tree-bark-colored tights.

- Where does the dog go after the ceremony? Is it sad when he's carried off, crying?

- Dog people are in fact crazier than cat people (dogs are more work, therefore they take up more headspace, therefore you are crazier for having one), and this act solidifies to your guests that you are not just the owner of a dog, but a full-blown "dog obsessive."

OTHER JOBS FOR ANIMALS:

- **Doggy Fortune Teller.** As your guests are exiting the venue, they will pass an elaborately decorated crate housing your dog, a sign that reads, "Con*FooFoo*fuscious says . . ." and a basket of fortunes. This is a fun send-off and a subtle way for your guests to see that your dog is cuter than theirs. Note: Could work with a cat, but they typically hate crates, and you don't want their meowing to bum the guests out.

- **Bird Ambiance-Maker.** If your theme is anything outdoors-y such as "Tropical Forest" or "Starry Starry Vineyard" or "Alice in Wonderland . . . with Birds," to kick things up a notch in terms of authenticity, let your pet bird fly around from flower arrangement to flower arrangement, centerpiece to occasional guest's shoulder. Sure, parakeets aren't considered "tropical" or "beautiful" or anything other than "depressing nursing home companion," but little Chirp Reynolds is available for parties. YOUR party. Just make sure he is trained like the hawk in *The Royal Tenenbaums* to come back to you at the end of the night. Also, he might poop all over the place. But, hey, that's the tropics for ya! A bummer? Or extreme, detailed execution of your theme?

- **Roamin' Roman Cats.** You and your fiancé got engaged during a trip to Italy, therefore you want your theme to be *"Multo Bongiorno!"* (Or whatever. I don't speak Italian). Point is, I've been to Rome, and I remember going to the ruins in the middle of the city, Largo di Torre Argentina, where they've had cats wandering around since Brutus unfriended Caesar. Why not incorporate this rich history into your reception?? It's not "gross" or "weird" to have random fur balls cowering under tables or strutting across the dance floor, it's Italiano! Plus, the stray cats *could* double as party favors for anybody who wants a cat or wants to look like a good person for the purposes of getting laid. Consider partnering with a local shelter.

- **Fish.** If you have a pet fish, exploit for use in a carnival game. Stick a sign near the bowl that says "Guess How Old He Is?" Whoever has the best guess wins: The prize is babysitting fishy while the couple goes on their honeymoon! (Really more of a win for the couple, but, hey, it's THEIR day.)

- **Wild Boar (or a dog that looks like one).** If you can secure one, set it up with some meat near the microphone to ward off any drunk guest who tries to grab the mic and sing during the reception.

VOW, bella!

"ACTIONS SPEAK LOUDER THAN WORDS." THIS IS, OF COURSE,
true. But vows are where you get to tell your partner what you will do, so
you can spend the rest of the marriage either doing it or accusing each
other of not doing it! It's a fun verbal contract, but with much more flow-
ery language. Although it would be amusing if you somehow worked in a
"Section B, Paragraph 12."

BIG BRIDAL SAYS: Writing your own vows is a
wonderful way to express yourself, while declaring
your love.

I SAY: If you don't write your own, just be prepared to
feel less connected, or possibly even zone out when
the pastor/rabbi/hot mess friend from college who
got certified on Officiant.com says generic, blanket
statements about "having" and "holding."

I wrote my vows two days before the wedding. If I had tried to write
them any sooner, they would have been angry with an undertone of re-

sentment towards Dan. I couldn't even focus on "our love." I completely lost sight of it during the Wedding Planning Process. But a few days before the wedding, I was blissed out, surrounded by family and friends and warm weather and staying in an idyllic, serene hotel. I was thrilled to write them. I was in the right frame of mind. I was in wedding mode. They poured out of me. I went to the little cafe at the hotel, refilled my iced coffee, plopped down at a picnic table wearing my big floppy hat and my brand-new chic-ass onesie and soaked up the sun while reflecting on what a wonderful experience I was having. People sat down at the table while I was writing the vows. My uncle Rob came by and I read him a little bit, to see what he thought.

I liked people stopping by while I was working on the vows. It was almost like a happy shiva. Or like I had a baby, and the village was coming by the house to bless the child. Only nobody brought food for me, the mother, to eat. But that's okay. I forgive their selfishness.

Going into the wedding I was dreading writing my vows because I was worried that as a performer, any kind of performance—even if it was just for Dan, technically—would feel like a stand-up set. I didn't want to "kill" in front of our comedian friends or "bomb" in front of them. I just wanted to be in the moment—hearing Dan, having him hear me, being together with glitter dust raining down around us like it does for Ariel when she kisses the prince in *The Little Mermaid*.

I wanted to make it personal, but I also wanted to hit the important points. In Seattle, you are not officially married unless you verbally declare during the ceremony that you take the person to be your spouse. I gotta say: I love this. I think it is important to say the basics because that's the constitution, the principles that define marriage, and your marriage. If you just read your vows and make jokes like "I promise to fold your underwear, even when they have stains on them" or whatever, you are being "funny" (and gross), but you are not cutting to the core, getting to the point, the whole reason you are there in the first place.

Also, overall our ceremony was a Grade-A clusterfuck in many ways. More on that later. In the end I am very glad I wrote my vows because it felt like the one thing I was able to control.

Here are my vows:

In order to get Dan here today I had to tell him this was a Wrestling podcast . . .

Dan, I love how you always live in the moment—just kidding. You are truly the most neurotic man I've ever met. You make Woody Allen look like Woody Harrelson, never chill, always looking forward. You always think about the future, which makes for an anxious human being, but a really wonderful partner! I love how you always think of me and our little family and strive to make our lives easier, better, and sweeter, from building us patio furniture to cooking us breakfast sandwiches every morning.

Conversely, I promise to donate my lack of foresight to every situation, to inject our relationship with my joie de vivre, which is French for "let's recklessly spend money on fun stuff"—I promise to make us step away from our routine of you sorting magic cards and me re-watching Black-fish for some sick reason and go out and see the world. Life is short, and we must fight to experience it to the fullest. That's where I come in. I promise to make us enjoy the present, to appreciate the ocean, the sand, the sun when we go to Cabo for our minimoon this coming Tuesday.

When you complain that the resort doesn't have large enough portions of eggs and that you need a certain amount of protein to retain your "killer physique," I will be there to remind you that we are lucky to be on an awesome vacation, celebrating each other and the love we share.

I promise to be "The Dan Whisperer"—to listen to you, to soothe you, to laugh with you, to be your best friend—like Dennis, but less furry.

You are the most supportive person I've ever met. If something good happens in my life, you are always a thousand times more excited for me than I could ever be, and I feel lucky to know that kind of love. You, Dan Black, have a heart of gold—bright gold—which perfectly matches the chain I am shocked you don't wear around your neck, considering you are basically a Soprano. You are the most Italian-feeling Jewish man I've ever met. Sometimes in my head I call you Jew-seppe.

I love that no matter what, you always have my back. You are my greatest ally—it is in your bones to protect and defend me—like the time our crazy racist neighbor yelled at my Uber driver because he was momentarily blocking our neighbor's driveway, you came out screaming, "Don't you dare scream at my fiancée!" You were a charged-up guido meatball and I loved it. I promise to be the same kind of meatball to you—just less loud. A daintier meatball, but a fiercely loyal one at that.

I love how smart you are—I love your perspective on life, your observations on the world around us—they're always interesting, witty

---

VOW WRITING TIPS

Have a friend read them and give honest feedback.

Avoid clichés. We know he is your best friend. We are not surprised that you are "partners in crime."

Actually say what you promise to do and be. Our rabbi did not make us repeat normal things like, "I will love you through thick and thin," and those things are important, they define marriage. So get that shit into your vows. It's almost like a job interview. But instead of lying, saying, "I'm a perfectionist," tell your partner what you will contribute to the company.

The more specific you are, the funnier it will be. Don't aim for hard jokes and punch lines. Seems forced. Specificity is funny and you don't have to try to be funny to pull it off. Saying the bride "loves to veg out and watch TV" isn't that funny. But saying the bride "watches every version of *Pride and Prejudice* back-to-back in her underwear" is . . . maybe funny, and way more authentic.

and eye-opening. You challenge and expand my thinking every day. I love the way you assume the position of, as I call it, "a low-stakes superhero"—you may not put on a cape and save people from a burning building, but you will perfectly articulate to Robert at Westlake Village Inn how it is classless to try and sell our wedding guests suites when plenty of standard rooms are still available.

Yesterday I looked up the definition of "vow," and Webster said it means: (a) an earnest promise, and (b) (and this was surprising) a threat to undertake.

Dan Black, I threaten to understand you, to be by your side through all of life's excitement as well as its monotony. To champion you. To be silly with you. To bring you up when you are down, to always roll my eyes when you tell me you have pink eye even though you don't, they're just vaguely red because you keep touching them. I threaten to change the lyrics of every song on the radio to make them about our Labradoodle . . . with you . . . to the tune of "Jealous" by Nick Jonas: "His name is Dennis."

You are one of the craziest, strangest, most difficult people I've ever met and I wouldn't have it any other way. But if you do want to change, I threaten to not object to that.

I love you, Fuzz, and thank you for loving a reallll pain in the ass . . . Me.

And until you write your own adorable declaration of love, here is your vow:

I vow to not minimize the importance of basic vows such as "to love and to cherish," etc. They're classics for a reason.

I also vow to use a thesaurus when I feel tempted to work the term "soul mate" into my speech. There's got to be another way to express our deep connection without this corniness.

Reception

PARTIES:
it's what themes are made of

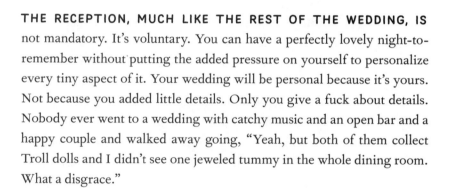

THE RECEPTION, MUCH LIKE THE REST OF THE WEDDING, IS not mandatory. It's voluntary. You can have a perfectly lovely night-to-remember without putting the added pressure on yourself to personalize every tiny aspect of it. Your wedding will be personal because it's yours. Not because you added little details. Only you give a fuck about details. Nobody ever went to a wedding with catchy music and an open bar and a happy couple and walked away going, "Yeah, but both of them collect Troll dolls and I didn't see one jeweled tummy in the whole dining room. What a disgrace."

> BIG BRIDAL SAYS: Ask yourself "What am I passionate about?" This is a good way to find your theme.

> I SAY: Well, let's see. My favorite pastimes are thinking people are mad at me, hoping I put on enough deodorant, and watching murder documentaries. Do those work?

My wedding theme was "My Wedding." It was in an outdoor botanical garden with birds and tea lights, so I let those do the "theme talking." I had flowers on the tables. That was it. I want to take a minute here to discuss the Big Bridal approach to theme-declaration because I hate it.

Big Bridal asks you "What do you do on weekends?" in order to help you figure out what you're "about." Well, we, as a couple, walk our dog, and sit around, and sometimes go to this Thai BBQ sports bar called The Hungry Pig, where we indulge in chicken wings and ribs and sometimes brisket and always mashed potatoes. Oftentimes I work, and he goes to the gym. Or I go to the gym, and he works. Should our favors at the end of the night be cookies shaped like barbells and laptops? No.

Point is, there needs to be a clear delineation between what is an acceptable passion to show off at your wedding (flowers, sequins, candles) and what's unacceptable (everything else).

The Knot says: "No matter what your passion is (be it taking long hikes in nature or watching football on the couch in the fall), there's gotta be something about it that you can use."

First of all, why do you need there to be "something about it that you can use"? Have you ever truly been to a wedding that felt like every detail was telling a story about the couple getting married? I've never been to a wedding that really *let me in*. They're all the same: food, band, booze, bye. The only wedding that was truly unique that I attended was impacted by a natural disaster, and I'm pretty certain that wasn't organized by the couple. "We want a wedding that's just electric . . . like struck by lightning!"

If a couple loves football, are you honestly charmed to find New York Giants memorabilia at their wedding? Does Vera Wang pair well with souvenir mugs shaped like helmets? Fucking of course not. If you and your fiancé love it, that's what counts. But the pressure to shoehorn details into your overall vibe and ambiance to say to your guests, "See? We like things together! We're so solid!" is overemphasis and overkill.

Another question posed in almost every wedding magazine is: "What expresses you as a couple?" I loathe this question. It is micro-aggressive, and guilts me and my fiancé into being less autonomous because somehow that is a weakness? In fact, Dan and I have very separate interests outside of each other. He loves playing Magic: The Gathering and watching wrestling. Should Dan come down the aisle to Stone Cold Steve Austin's theme song? (Dan did suggest this . . .) I respectfully hate both of his passions. I like working, watching shows on Netflix, and other than that my life is mostly errands and taking care of Dennis. I used to like art—making it and seeing it—but lately it has been low on the priority list.

This is why everyone sticks with floral decor, popular music, and lots of alcohol. They are not divisive. No couple has ever been in a heated debate, like, "Fuck flowers!" They're the Switzerland of the wedding world.

One thing Dan and I have been bonding over lately is the Showtime series *The Affair* . . . which is literally ALL about cheating. In fact, I saw Joshua Jackson once when I was at Sirius Radio, and he was shocked when I told him that I watch the show with my soon-to-be-husband. But I think we can all agree incorporating a show

NEW THEME IDEAS I WOULD ACTUALLY LOVE TO SEE

"No Makeup Wedding." Nobody, bride included, is allowed to wear makeup. Let's all remove our masks and be the purest versions of ourselves. Regular weddings, it's like, "He loves me for me." I mean, but you're wearing a strip of giant lashes and foundation not only on your face but also on your body? "I'm doing it for the pictures!" But the pictures aren't even of you. You're buried under five pounds of war paint. You'd look more like yourself wearing one of those head-to-toe fuzzy chicken costumes.

"Sweatpants Wedding." UGG slippers optional. Stains optional. Bride and groom will save on napkins because guests can wipe hands off on thighs.

"Spanx Wedding." We all strip down to the undergarments that shape our bodies into lies and celebrate that none of us are actually photoshopped. We are flawed diamonds. Note: Men have to wear man Spanx, those shape-wear tanks, even if they don't need them. Out of solidarity.

"Horror Wedding." Bride drags herself down the aisle as the final girl in a slasher flick, like she's just made it out of the woods and is flagging down the groom in his car.

Through cuisine! Take chances. Just make sure you have enough food. Quantity is important when you are essentially holding people hostage for five hours. You know how Maggiano's Little Italy or The Cheesecake Factory has offensive portion sizes? Strive for that. Nothing kills a food boner faster at a wedding than: "Sorrrrryyy, we ran out of the salmon. Want some pity carbs? We've got plenty of rice left over because, well, this is LA, and people hate when their mouths and stomachs experience bliss."

Through music! The songs you play while people are arriving can be pretty much whatever you want because there is no pressure for people to dance at that point.

Through your vows. Within reason.

Speeches made by parents and/or siblings. This doesn't inform who you are as a couple, but it does let the guests into your individual worlds a little more. "Who birthed these shit-shows? Oh, *they* did? This adds up."

about infidelity into our wedding on any level would be troubling.

The Knot reminds us, "Let creativity flow. Put your personal stamp on all of the details." Sure, it is cute when details reflect your personal taste, but it is also cute when the bathrooms are clean, and the food isn't horrible. People just want *nice*. Not quirky, not "They really outdid themselves!" Just, "That was thoughtful." By all means, if you love DIY projects, do it up. Make a collage out of corks! Go for it! But the pressure to "make it your own" with every little wedding detail is just silly. You notice your efforts. Your guests do not.

Tip: If you like the idea of DIY, but don't actually want to DIY, have a bridesmaid DIT (do it themselves)! My bridesmaid, Mary, made candied pecans for my wedding favors. She's a fabulous mother with two kids and honestly found it to be fun to help in a way that was creative and not just responding to me barking "Carry this!" and "Where's my phone?" Plus, I slaved over flower-shaped butter mints for her wedding, so she owed me.

Determine the Formality

There's also a lot of pressure around DTF, ya'll!!! No, it doesn't mean you're hornier than Diane Keaton at a turtleneck convention. It means Determine the Formality. Big Bridal tells you to figure out how fancy you want things to be first, but I think this is counterintuitive. The DTF realization will happen for you through two other decisions: Dress + Venue = Formality. When you try on wedding dresses, you know when you've found the one. Same goes for venue, pretty much. So if you can narrow down the venue, and then get your dress, you will know the formality. This is not something you need to know in advance, because you might think you want a black-tie ballroom affair, then come to realize the ballroom actually feels like a conference room off the lobby of an Atlantic City casino: Dingy carpet that wreaks of smoke and sad grannies on Rascal scooters. No, thanks. Not at my wedding.

An Affair to Remember

The most annoying Big Bridal advice of all is to "make your wedding memorable." What do they expect? Should you request that, before your guests attend the wedding, they complete a book of Sudoku to make sure their memory is as sharp as possible? One Sudoku won't do it. Have a drop box for the completed Sudoku books at the entrance. And if any of the pages are blank, you can mail those to the guests along with their thank-you note. A sharp brain *after* the wedding is also important. Long-term memories must be made. The obsession with memorable weddings is a bit pathological, but let's go for it.

- Make sure your wedding is the only wedding anyone ever attends ever again. Kill all of the other engaged people in your guests' lives. Go to prison! Jumpsuit orange is so your color!

- Have something catch on fire during your ceremony. OR, release some kind of airborne toxin.

- Get in a huge fight with your husband, in front of everyone. Make the DJ actually record-scratch to a halt upon witnessing the confrontation.

You can't control the lasting impression you leave on your guests, so stop worrying about your wedding being burned into their brains. This isn't *Memento*. They'll remember what they want to remember and block out what they choose to block out. That is their prerogative.

 *I vow to let my guests remember what they want to remember and block out what they want to block out.*

MENU
can do it

I FEEL LIKE THERE'S A REAL SPLIT WHEN IT COMES TO CONCERN over food at weddings. You either hear "Food doesn't matter. You just want everyone to be up and dancing. Nobody goes to weddings for the food." OR you hear "All I care about is having good food." It's a matter of taste, which makes sense. Some of us live to eat, others eat to live, and yet we all are expected to party together.

BIG BRIDAL SAYS: **Go local and go seasonal.**

I SAY: **Suuuure, but also mac-n-cheese is a pretty powerful crowd-pleaser.**

Me personally? I'm in the camp of "Let there be quantity." Not because that's what I think matters, but because my man is from Long Island and they are known for their over-the-top catering hall weddings, with heaps of food from around the world. Ever see sushi in mass quantity? Have you ever wanted to? Of course not. But too bad because if you're at a Long Island wedding, you're gonna see heaps. As much as I poke fun at the catering hall obsession with quantity, I also get where they're coming from. When you go to a wedding, it's a little like being shipwrecked on an island. You're trapped in a strange place with strange people, slipping you into survival mode. "When will we get to eat? Will we ever get to eat? Will I have to climb up a tree to pick bananas? Will a coconut fall on my head and bop me unconscious?" The reason for survival mode is because we've all been duped before. We've all gone to the wedding with the longer-than-it-needed-to-be ceremony followed by the "I-only-caught-one-phyllo-spinach-triangle" from a cater waiter who passed apps during cocktail hour. This is why I think it's fun to surprise guests not with the *best* bruschetta they've ever *tasted*, but the *most* bruschetta they've ever *wanted*.

My Food Rules

1. YOU'RE VEGAN—I'M NOT

My friend had a Southern Indian vegetarian wedding, and the food was exquisite. A wedding Dan and I went to in Houston served "Mexican vegan cuisine" and it was all chips and rice, i.e., a bloat fest, a *cheap* bloat fest. Look, I'm not saying MEAT = HAPPINESS. I can experience your outlook on food for a night without pitching a fit, I'm not a child. But when I see meat, I think, "Oh, yay, a chance at feeling full without feeling gross." Pasta-starch full is not the same kind of full as meat-and-veggies full. IF you want to provide a menu that is diverse with various types of dishes containing different types of substitute non-animal proteins, I will let you take me on a tour of the foods that really rock your world. But I will likely get a hamburger on my way home afterwards.

2. FOOD BEFORE THE CEREMONY

Why is cocktail hour the first time people get to eat at your wedding? Dan and I put out iced coffee and strawberry bruschetta before our ceremony so people would feel equal parts amped up on caffeine, confused as to WTH is "strawberry bruschetta???," and happy to just put anything in their mouths before the ceremony—whether it be a weird appetizer, melon balls, human balls, whatever. Just something to satiate. It sets the tone of "We care. Thank you for being here. You will not be hungry. We've *got* you."

3. WE KNOW WHEN YOU'RE BEING CHEAP

When Dan and I first started dating, we went to a Saturday night wedding that didn't serve dinner. They circulated cold cocktail shrimp and sliders. And later cupcakes. That's IT. When you scale back on food, people notice. Downgrading plates, china, that kind of nonsense—nobody will ever care. But when they're only eating rice and beans like they're on a camping trip minus the woods, lake, scenery, and compelling ghost stories/imminent fear of bears/Lyme's disease/ghosts from the stories coming to life, they're gonna know you tried to save money. There's nothing embarrassing about saving money *except* when it directly impacts your guests' fuel levels. They need fuel. *You trapped them. You feed them.*

4. BUFFETS ARE NOT TRASHY

They are cheaper, without compromising the quality of the food. Doing a plated dinner is usually more expensive than serving the exact same food at a buffet. So go buffet! People like being able to take as much or as little as they want. Again, quantity puts people at ease at weddings. They want to feel like they won't go hungry after being marooned on Wedding Island. Sure, buffets are not the classiest, but they are the funnest. Cici's Pizza? Great restaurant. Those Chinese buffets with lo mein but also chicken tenders and fries and surprisingly decent cheesecake? Sign me up. If your wedding can light up the happy buffet part of my brain, I will, no question, enjoy it 20 percent more than other weddings, just based on the excitement of standing in line, scooping, moving to the next station, scooping. Taking two rolls 'cuz, fuck it, they're in a basket, not being doled out with a silver tong by a dead-eyed waitress in a bowtie . . . I'm IN.

5. EVERYONE HATES TAPAS

Not doing a sit-down dinner but instead just passing around sliders . . . Unacceptable. You know what happens when someone eats a slider? They start doing math. "How many sliders do I have to catch from the cater waiters to equal one full burger?" The answer is: A LOT. Because even if you eat six sliders, your brain will not say, "Okay, I'm full." You're in Snacking Mode. Technically, you might be full, but your brain is screaming, "Feed her more!" The great thing about a buffet or plated dinner is that it signals to our dumb unquenchable brains, "You ate. Now you dance." If your guests are slow-chasing the guy with the shrimp like the cops chased O.J. in the Bronco, sure, it might make people mingle more, but all they'll talk about is FOOD. Not an interesting article on helicopter parenting. Not the surprisingly good documentary you saw about Alice Cooper, even though you were never a fan, but now you are—still not of his music, but of him as a person. Nothing deep or edgy or dark or of substance. *No sustenance. No substance.* That's what I always (just now) say. People will mingle no matter how you serve the food. Don't reinvent the wheel. Dinner—sitting, eating, focusing, chewing, stabbing meat with a fork, chewing more—it works. It has always worked. If it ain't broke, don't fix it.

6. CAKES: PERMISSION TO KEEP IT SIMPLE

I thought designing a cake would be really important to me, as I've always been a huge cake Pinterester and a fan of Food Network's *Ace of Cakes* . . . But when it came down to it, getting a simple inexpensive cake versus one that is a detailed 3-D portrait of our Labradoodle was the best move for us. Nobody *really* cares about your wedding cake. It's just a fun thing to cut and destroy. That's like having a lavish, intricate Jenga tower . . . like, what's the point? My mom made the cake topper, and it was very special. And kind of big. Think diorama: It included a miniature toy version of my Prius, and figurines of Dennis, Dan, and myself. The cake people were annoying and suggested it didn't look professional. I was concerned until I remembered my wedding is not a corporate new-product kickoff.

 *I vow to not skimp on quantity of food. It's rude. It's the only thing a guest could complain about and be totally in the right.*

MUSIC: everyone's got an opinion

LIKE I SAID, NO ONE THING CAN MAKE OR BREAK A WEDDING, but one thing that can come pretty mutherfudgin' close is bad music. This doesn't mean that you have to play only pop music. But do not forget: "pop" is short for popular. And "soda" in the Midwest. Soda songs might not be the thing you play into your earbuds when you're trying to avoid Greenpeace stopping you on the sidewalk with their guilt propaganda about "saving the environment" or "helping children" or WHATEVER. But they are effective for getting a party going. Sure, if you're determined to hire that Ben Folds Five cover band called Ben Folds Four (which is ironic because it's just one guy named Newton—not Ben—who plays the drum, harmonica, and a keyboard simultaneously, like a New Orleans street performer), I am not here to say don't hire them. But do be aware that the gimmick will wear off fast—faster than your lip "stain." P.S. Makeup tips to come later!

BIG BRIDAL SAYS: Play classic tunes that all age groups can enjoy to ensure that all your guests get their groove on.

I SAY: Do you think that if there are people over fifty at your wedding, and you don't play a Pandora-style selection of Earth, Wind & Fire, or the like, you'll cause a Shit, Storm & Shit Storm? Wrong. Everybody can appreciate the dance hits of the day.

People tend to think, "Older guests want to feel like they're in a commercial for a Disney cruise, step-touching to 'Celebration,' not doing body rolls to Fetty Wap! Right?" Wrong.

My ninety-four-year-old grandpa sat down at my cousin's wedding UNTIL Rihanna came on. He didn't give a shit about "The Way You Look Tonight." He wanted to shake his sag-tastic rump for two and half minutes without having young people come over and tell him how "good" he looks. (He finds it condescending that people obsess over how "sharp" he is considering his age.)

We were going to have this young hip band (the group's mean age was twenty-three) that covered new songs—like cool-and-unusual new, not just Top-40-bar-mitzvah new—but Dan's parents insisted on this fuddy-duddy older white Jewish gentleman named Pinkus, with a straight-up auburn hair piece, and I was, like, "Sure." He came to my house and borrowed Dan's guitar and jammed out on our porch. Was it that impressive? No, but I appreciated the effort, our very own private *Pinkus Unplugged* concert. He sang AT ME. He held my gaze while tenderly crooning the classic chorus, "Don't stop believing . . ." I wanted to look away, but then came, "Hold on to that feeling . . ." It was like a game of chicken: whoever is the first to break eye contact with Pinkus clearly has intimacy issues.

Ultimately, I don't regret my decision to have a band (because I don't believe in wedding regret, more on that later . . .), but the band did not sound good. The mixing was off—the guitar was much louder than the vocals . . . which maybe was a good thing because what I heard of the vocals was rough.

Wedding bands usually have one or two powerhouse Aretha Franklin clones, amazing talents that span far beyond working the wedding circuit, but there is always an embarrassing element to the rest of the group. Whether it's a sax player wearing a plaid vest and matching plaid bowtie because he wants to "look like a hipster" or the old "he's still got it!" front man who actually doesn't still "got it." Unless "it" is visible hair plugs. Try to go see the band in action before you book them, because while many groups have music videos online, they have usually been heavily produced. Not only are all the flaws removed, but oftentimes the people in the video are not the ones who show up to play at your wedding.

If it's any comfort, I went to a wedding that had a Spotify playlist on somebody's phone plugged into a speaker, and honestly, I didn't even notice that there wasn't a DJ until the text message alert interrupted "Thriller."

That said, if you don't hire a DJ, you do have to appoint someone who can man or wo-man an iPod. Don't just hand that job to your friend who isn't a bridesmaid but is hungry for a task. Make sure it's someone who can deal with cords and volume and . . . cords. And speakers. And cords. Cords are my 'Nam. Even if there're only two or three, they remind me of that scene in *National Lampoon's Christmas Vacation,* the giant messy ball of Christmas lights. "Untangle these, Russ."

DJ is my favorite option. It's just a safe bet. A good DJ will double as an MC, who can keep the flow of the party going, make announcements like "Please welcome the bride and groom" and "Dinner is now served" and "Be careful when you do the Electric Slide, Uncle Pat. You just had hip surgery and caught a handy J from the cater waiter in the bathroom. Go easy."

A good DJ also can play, not a cover of your favorite song, but your *actual favorite song*. Dan's and my first dance was to "All I Want Is You" by U2 because *Reality Bites* is one of my favorite movies and that song plays over the Winona/Ethan Hawke montage. It's a beautiful song. But when Pinkus "sang" it, it sounded like *UWho?* It completely lost its essence, its pacing, its Bono-ness.

Dan believes that "nothing gets a party going like live music." When I brought up having a DJ, he pouted like a puppy. He said, "Nobody sits down when a live band is playing right in front of them." That's simply untrue. People, who want to sit, will sit. My mom and several members of my dad's family stayed seated, looking at nonsense on their phones (not sure what, but there was scrolling happening when I looked over, so I hope it was a really juicy celeb sex tape to justify how checked-out they were), during the bulk of the dancing at our wedding. I was momentarily bothered, but, on a sociological level, pleased to prove my point that people who don't want to dance are not going to dance.

New music, familiar music, is best. I'm not saying "Celebration" doesn't have its place at weddings. Actually I *am* saying it. I never get excited to hear it, and I don't think other people get that excited. I actually think it is a buzz kill. Plus, when you play those "step touch" songs, you become acutely aware of your whiteness and that leads to guilt and nobody needs guilt at a wedding other than the Jewish kind. Play music that is upbeat, current, and cutting-edge. Splash in the oldies if you must, like you splash cran into vodka to drunkenly stave off a UTI.

If your band has a gimmick, like mullets and they only cover '80s rock that you usually only hear at strip clubs, make sure you are booking them because that's the music you really want to dance to, not because you feel pressure to have people walking away going, "That was so different." Different for the sake of different is boring. If you want to really be different, forget music altogether! Big Bridal is all about standing out, making your wedding unforgettable, so if you want to go that route, rrrrreally go for it. How about sounds of whales, sonar technology–style, just deep outcries between a mother whale and its baby? You can put on the invites, "*Blackfish* Tie Optional."

I'd recommend you do not pay close attention to song lyrics, pay attention to tempo and melody. Plenty of amazing songs have terribly depressing lyrics, lyrics that go against the very idea of love and marriage and togetherness, but does that mean they don't get played at the wedding? Fuck no. Robyn's "Dancing on My Own"? That gem gets people on the dance floor faster than a coupon will get my mother-in-law to Costco, and the lyrics are about being in the corner, watching your crush kiss another girl, knowing you won't be the one he takes home, and then just saying "screw it" and dancing . . . on your own. Yet this go-to party anthem makes everyone throw their hands in the air like they do not care, forgetting that the song is kind of stalker-ish, and that many of us will likely be going home alone (but not *this* broad! She's all wifed up!). One of Robyn's other songs, "Call Your Girlfriend," is all about a breakup. But my friend Kara, who had the best wedding I've ever been to, at a summer camp in Vermont, had both Robyn songs on her playlist, and it was nothing short of a slammin' good time.

I'd also suggest you play your weird personal favorites while people are taking their seats or during cocktail hour. If you're like me and have quirky music taste, no problem. Pre-ceremony and cocktail hour are two inconsequential times when you can showcase who you are through music. Bust out those deep-cut B-sides that make you feel like a cool preteen who knows cool music that loser adults know nothing about. My parents were concert promoters when I was a kid, so I grew up listening to bands right before they got big. I am a music snob. I love Indie rock and '80s New Wave, groups like New Order and Joy Division. But do guests want to cut a rug to the haunting voice of Ian Curtis warbling "She's lost control"? I mean, I would, but that's not the point. Save it for the shuffle to the seats or eating-ceviche-out-of-a-shotglass chitchat time.

The wedding reception is about *giving back*. Friends and family sat through your ceremony, they mingled during cocktail hour having mind-numbing conversations ("You're from Delaware? So funny, my neighbor has a fleece pullover from the Dover airport!"), and now they've made it to the main event. Give the guests what they musically need: familiarity. Or semi-familiarity (e.g., Icona Pop's "I Love It," the Ting Tings' "That's Not My Name"—songs that people have heard, even though they might not know who sings them). Sure, pepper in a few of your esoteric favs, but be prepared for people to sit down when they hear them. A peppering is fine. A sprinkle. Not the other side of the spice opening that allows you to just dump the seasoning on the tilapia. The one with the three holes that makes it come out slowly, safely, with caution.

Whatever music source I choose, I will prioritize danceability.

SPEECHY keen

ONE THING IS CERTAIN: THERE WILL BE SPEECHES, GIVEN BY people with no real ability for public speaking, who finally get their chance to possibly ruin your whole night. Do not leave it up to them to do whatever they want because, although they are the people closest to you, they are probably huge dopes. Here is a list of rules you can give the best man, MoH, and any parents stepping up to the mic to ensure the spotlight stays on you.

> **BIG BRIDAL SAYS: Don't talk about how drunk they got in college or what kind of trouble they used to get into.**
>
> **I SAY: You can talk about anything, as long as it's specific, funny, and relevant to a point. We're all adults.**

Dan said to me at his friend's rehearsal dinner, "Girls' speeches are never as funny as the guys' speeches." I, of course, told him that was sexist, but he (somewhat) justified his point. Girl friendships and guy friendships have one major difference, which is that guys call each other on their bullshit, girls do not. Guys aren't afraid of each other, girls are.

He is right—girls' speeches are usually a little more reeled in, laden with strings of positive adjectives. "She's kind, funny, loyal, sweet . . ." while guys will straight up say, "How the fuck did this fat dingbat ever land a piece of ass like Judy?" It's stupid, yes, but it always gets a laugh.

I'm not saying guys are better at speeches than girls. Hardly. But I *am* saying guys can learn from the girls, and girls can learn from the guys. Guys, soften it up a bit. Girls, don't be timid. I wanted my girlfriends' speeches to go deep, to actually reveal that we are in fact more than surface friends. It feels nice to remember that your friends *see* you.

I vow to not feel offended when my bridesmaid roasts me.

I sent this e-mail to the groomsmen and bridesmaids, but really it was for the groomsmen, and I felt so bitchy for sending it. Nobody wrote back, which is an automatic sign that they thought I was a tool for even broaching the subject.

Hey bros & babes!
So excited to celebrate with you all so sooooon! Yay!!!
Quick heads up about the rehearsal dinner: If you would like to speak at the dinner, we'd love to hear from you! Got a little microphone and amp and everything. Cute! Just try to keep it short-ish, and let's err on the side of not roasting so hard that it knocks the air out of the room and makes my grandpa have a war flashback.

Love you all, can't wait to see you in a few weeks!
Hugs, kisses and incredibly sensual sexts,
Jamie

So okay, maybe, maybe loosen the reins on the speeches. But feel free to leave this page open when your MoH comes over to help you glue moss to foam cutouts of your and your fiancé's initials for the gift table.

No rapping. Unless your maid of honor is Missy Elliot, tell her to play out her hip-hop fantasies elsewhere. Don't even think of doing a Fresh Prince of Bel-Air parody. For some reason this is the MoH go-to, and it just turns into a monotone list of personal details with a '90s sitcom theme song playing in the background, and usually the beat boxer drags on the beat.

No viral video attempts. YouTube wedding videos have made some think that a wedding speech is their time to get famous. Flash mobs are an embarrassment. If you start giving your speech and my cousin stands up and starts singing, it better be because she is disgustingly drunk.

Lean into jokes. Women, you are funny. Don't let the guys be the only roasters.

Tighten it up. You know what nobody gives a shit about? When I, the bride, first told you about the groom. It's the same story every time and of course you remember it . . . it happened three years ago. Want to see a room full of people check their phones? Tell the harrowing tale of when you first heard about my fiancé, and how you thought he sounded great or terrible. Or how I finally seemed happy.

Reel in the basic bitchiness of it all. At a family friend's wedding, one bridesmaid got up and told this story about how she and the bride had eaten cupcakes together and it ended with "I love how you love dessert." It was just the most vapid thing ever, and told the rehearsal dinner attendees nothing about the bride. My mom leaned over and said, "Who the fuck doesn't love dessert?" Inane comments like this don't let us into your and the bride's world together, your dynamic, your importance to each other. In fact, they just set women back. You sound like you're a man doing an impression of "women" in a really bad stand-up routine. Women *love* *dessert* isn't a far cry from women *be shoppin'*. Embrace your femininity, yes. But represent your gender in a way that tells us how cool and complex female friendships are.

Tears are sweet. Hysterical tears are not. At my rehearsal dinner, one of my bridesmaids gave a speech, by which I mean she took the microphone and immediately started sobbing. No, not because she had an overwhelming wave of excitement and affection towards Dan and me. She was talking about her journey toward self-acceptance, and just lost it. My friend Kate is sitting at my table next to me, squeezing my bicep, horrified. "This is so narcissistic, I can't even take it," she whispered. In the moment, I actually thought the meltdown was sweet. "Awww, she's so emotional. That's *emotional* snot dripping from her nose onto the mic that others have to use." But later I pondered Kate's perception and concluded, "Emotional does not mean heartfelt." This goes for both the bridesmaids and groomsmen: The speech should be about the couple. Both of them. The whole speech.

Now for the best man. Your fiancé has likely chosen a best man who is probably a fine person, but for some reason the microphone makes men feel like everything they say is funny and interesting. They need a little guidance. Have your future husband hand off these guidelines to his BM. (Best Man. Yes, it's the same acronym as Bowel Movement. Coincidence? Only you know the answer to that.) It's better if it looks like it's his words to his friend, not your recommendations, so you don't come off as controlling, which you aren't, except at your frigging wedding:

We weren't that crazy in college. Sure, we did some drinking at UMass, but it was pretty mild. We did graduate. If we were really crazy in college, we'd be in jail or at the very least sober now and too scared to talk about the dark days. Cut the stupid college stories where you act like we were unusually wild, more so than others.

Brother, don't be a dick. Yes, siblings have embarrassing stories to tell from childhood, now STFU. If you want to talk about the time that I crapped my pants on the class trip to the aquarium, I will tell everyone about that baloney sandwich you practiced sex on.

There were no other girls. Whatever the context, do not talk about the last girlfriend. We all know she exists, but if the bride hears her name, your mic is getting cut off. The only circumstances where it would be okay to mention her:

- She is a convicted killer. Everyone loves true crime, and that is just a gripping story to tell.

- She is the reason you and your husband met. And she is at the wedding with her new husband. It worked out for everyone.

No jokey jokes. Sorry, you're not funny. Yes, I know you believe in your heart that you are. Guess who else thinks they're funny? Every man. Almost all of them are wrong. Yes, the maid of honor gets one joke, but I trust her more than you to not say "fuckin'" twenty times. If you must joke, run your speech by someone who doesn't love you to get an honest reaction. Your buddy is not an okay test group.

Just be nice. All you have to say is that we look great, we love each other, and then wish us a life full of happiness. DONE. See how easy that is? There's no such thing as a too short best man speech—if it's short, everyone loves it. And if you are trying to have sex with one of the bridesmaids, a short simple speech won't screw it up.

Tip for everyone: make it about the couple as much as possible. For example: MoH, if you spend the majority of the speech talking about you and the bride and your amazing backpacking trip through Budapest, loop it back to the groom somehow. "Simon is like a Hungarian dessert: strange, multilayered, but also very rich."

Run it by a friend. An educated friend who will give you honest feedback. Parents will always be more embarrassing to their children than their friends. You have to work extra hard to eliminate anything that could cause cringing, uncomfortable rosacea blushing, excessive bridal boob sweat, etc.

Your age is not a crutch. It's a beautiful thing that as you get older you give less of a fuck, but in this instance, you should. Don't wing it so hard that you end up laughing in the middle, taking side trips, detouring, stopping off at rest stops along the way before eventually getting back on the main road. We don't want to hear about the groom's "Pepé Le Pew–themed" bar mitzvah. Then, a portrait of the groom in high school. Then, college. What is this, a PowerPoint presentation at a community center? No. Unless the groom met the bride at the bar mitzvah (She was dressed as Petunia Pig!), then stuff it. Get to the both of us, or get out.

The story about when the bride was little or the groom was little is only cute if it has a point that ties back to the couple. Otherwise it's just an embarrassing show-and-tell and you chose "When Michael peed his bunk at summer camp and they insisted on giving him rubber sheets." Just because it was a long time ago doesn't mean it's cuter now that it's a vintage tale.

Psychology

(BRIDOPATHY)

PLANNING
and stress

I WOULD LIKE TO START THIS SECTION OFF BY SAYING HOW much I hate the term "Bridezilla." A bride is not a malevolent dinosaur who eats people and climbs buildings like a squirrel climbs trees. It's almost a (much less harmful or consequential) slur at this point. I put it on the same level as calling a strong, driven woman "pushy," or an opinionated woman "mouthy." I much prefer the term "Bridopath." The stress and emotional complexity around wedding planning is an illness, and we should be sensitive to it. This shit is hard.

Planning for a wedding is hours upon hours of reading into the significance of details that no one will ever notice until you point out to your cousin that you made the bridesmaids wear a purple ribbon in their hair in memory of the great grandmother who choked to death on a grape that she tried to swallow whole on a bar bet.

BIG BRIDAL SAYS: Try yoga!

I SAY: Fuck you.

First, purchase a copy of *The Knot Complete Guide to Weddings* and tear it in half—the binding will be tough, but you want that resistance to make the ripping satisfying. It might seem like a waste of money, but for eleven dollars, it might be worth the money you'll save by not buying everything those shills are selling.

Regarding details anxiety, yes, they are what make the day special, but be completely ready for nobody to give a shit about how hard it was to find the perfect flower petals to spread on tables at the reception or that the groomsmen are wearing cummerbunds with their tuxedoes because of some ethnic tradition that you read about.

Much like vacation photos and sex stories, they are only for bragging rights, and whoever has to hear about them kind of hates you for a moment. The point is, the details that you can enjoy all by yourself are the only ones that matter. If you read it on Martha Stewart Weddings or some other bullshit bridal site, ignore it.

If you're considering doing something you think is "weird," and you need a confidence boost, try googling it. If you're thinking you might want to get married without a ring, then try googling "I got married with no ring"—lots of cool, attractive chicks have no doubt done it, so it might inspire you.

Cleanse your stress palate during the Wedding Planning Process with these strangely cathartic gems!

Law & Order. Your florist died, and you have to find a new one in one week's time . . . But at least you don't have to solve the case. The legal system is more of a mess than your special day will ever be!

Splash. This movie is an atrocity well worth watching again to see exactly why. It's the least feminist love story of all time. A mermaid-turned-naked-woman stumbles around, Tom Hanks finds her and thinks he's in love (because she's naked), she can't form a sentence, but she is horny as hell so she's "the woman of his dreams." It is a love story so shallow it will make you feel amazing about your upcoming marriage no matter how much you and your fiancé are fighting.

Sixteen Candles. When you rewatch this classic you will be so shocked at the rapey-ness of the scene where Jake Ryan "hands over" his passed-out girlfriend to the freshman so he can "take her home." Wink, wink. It is utterly disturbing and will replace any thought of "I hope my maid of honor doesn't feel put out."

The Genius of Marian. A documentary about a brilliant artist who is losing her cognitive ability due to early onset Alzheimer's. It's a beautiful story that makes you appreciate what you have, which is a lot if you are reading this book and you at least had twenty bucks or whatever to purchase it. Maybe your friend read it and passed it down to you? At least you have a friend who happens to think of things you would like. Maybe you found this book lying in a dank puddle with dick graffiti drawn on it . . . Be thankful that it rains where you live! In LA, where I live, there's a drought. Lots to be thankful for. Take a breather from wedding planning. Appreciate.

Giada at Home. She's just blissful. A goddess woman with a big white smile and a great attitude, which is completely fake—nobody is thrilled about *re-coat-ta* the way she pretends to be, but her lack of reality allows you to escape your reality, of wedding stress. Cooking shows in general are a great escape because (a) food is awesome, (b) watching food is much less low calorie than eating it, and (c) on most cooking shows they don't even acknowledge nutrition, let alone calories. They just go balls-out, saying, "We're making lasagna because it tastes great!" No cooking show has ever started with "Ugh, we're being bad, but . . ." It's always just "Butter is great! Let's use as much as possible because it's perfect!"

Chef's Table. Netflix documentary series profiling the world's best chefs. It's less about the food and more about the origin story: Every person in this documentary is obsessed with where they're from and wants to incorporate their background and upbringing into their food. Their parents got a divorce? They want the risotto to taste like divorce! It's inspirational to see people who know they can't choose their family or where they're from, and wouldn't want to. It's the opposite of how most people feel when they're planning a wedding.

DOUBTS: TO HAVE. TO HOLD.
to question.

PLANNING A WEDDING IS ALL ABOUT THE SEMI-SUPERFICIAL; other than religious choices or vows, it's a party. That's all well and good, but the fact that it takes place while you are in the midst of adjusting to a major life change, which is essentially a bet, makes things challenging. I'd say Make Space for Doubt.

"How did you know he was the one?" people ask. I say, "When I was thirty-two and not married."

For some reason we're not allowed to acknowledge that part of wanting to get married is social pressure. A large part. It's not the whole reason, but at the very least you have had a grandmother say something undercutting that really got under your skin. "When are you settling down?" she asked, while you watched her eat cottage cheese with her mouth open at Golden Corral.

It's called settling down because there is an element of settling . . . downward. It doesn't mean you don't love your partner, it doesn't mean you are giving up, but it does mean that in taking things to the next level, you are saying "au revoir" to your single-person status officially. It should be called "evolving" or "growing together," but come on: When all of your friends start getting married at the age of twenty-eight to thirty-three, is that just coincidence? Or is there an element of settling? The latter is true, and it's okay!

If you've been together awhile, it's nice to get those people off your back, the ones who keep asking when you're "taking the plunge," or some other equally harrowing metaphor. I'm the weak asshole who can't handle any questioning, so I just chose marriage because it was easier than not choosing it. And because I love Dan! But acting like society doesn't play a role in my wanting to find "the one" is "just silly."

But so it doesn't have a negative connotation, let's call it SETTLING UP, not settling down.

I'm settling up, not settling down.

This makes marriage sound like a positive evolution versus you tobogganing on a downward slope into a tar pit. We've entered a weird time in society where breaking up is not only common, but oftentimes proof of strength, independence, knowing what you want, shedding your cocoon to emerge a butterfly. Just as society pressures us to join the married club, they praise us for our bravery as we pull a Beyoncé and tell that loser to step to the left (to the left).

My cousin, who got engaged shortly after I did, was supposed to get married the July after my wedding. He and his fiancée seemed to have this indefectible love for each other. They were affectionate, not in the nauseating way, but in the way where I would compare Dan and me to them. "Dan only puts his arm around me, he doesn't stroke my cheek like that."

Crazy minutia I would obsess over because I thought, "That's the perfect couple." She was into art, he was into sports, yet somehow they really had this yin-yang, opposites attract thing working for them.

A month before my wedding, I missed three calls from my aunt Dana. Finally we got on the phone. I was nervous . . . Dana said, "Are you sitting down?" I was worried something had happened to my grandpa. "Yes. Well, I'm driving. That's a form of sitting. Tell me. What's up?"

"Mitch and Sadie broke off the engagement."

My mouth dropped to the floor, my face went white, I almost rear-ended the guy in front of me in traffic. How could the poster children for LOVE not be getting married?

Not only that—now Sadie is all over Instagram hanging out with some new guy named Thad (who looks like a total Thad), and we all think maybe she cheated on my cousin . . . It's just the old cliché of "Nothing is at it seems." You can never think you know a relationship, the ins and outs of it, the grit of it, unless you are in fact in that relationship yourself.

I called Dan after I got the news, and he was not that shocked. Then I got annoyed that he wasn't more shocked, but he said, "You always compare our relationship to other people's and you shouldn't."

This really resonated with me . . . I do form opinions of other couples based on outward evidence, like how affectionate they are, how they talk to each other, how happy they *seem*. I think it's because of romantic comedies—we've trained our brains to believe that if two people are acting anything remotely like a couple in a romantic comedy, that's because their life *is* a romantic comedy, full of nonstop laughter and joy and sex and epic "no YOU hang up" phone calls. Meanwhile the romantic comedy couple in my life, Mitch and Sadie, fell apart, and the goofy Long Island Guido/ Dallas Jewess (come to think about it, Dan and I *should* be in a rom com) have been together six years and are about to get married.

I realized when Mitch and Sadie broke up that a lot of my doubts about my relationship were out of *comparison* to other couples, and that what I was comparing my relationship to was just a *perception* of someone else's relationship, not a reality.

I will catch myself in the act of comparing the actualities of my relationship to the perceptions I have of other people's relationships.

Of course, not every struggle comes out of comparison. Sometimes you're just straight up in the shit of a fight and not thinking about anyone else. Two weeks before our wedding, Dan and I fought outside the jewelers when we were picking up the wedding bands. It was the kind of hostile verbal altercation where passersby stop and stare, thinking, "Should I intervene?" What was it about? What *wasn't* it about? At that point, it felt like if I didn't do what Dan and his parents wanted, he would pick a fight with me. He wanted everyone to get along, to please his parents, but my wants and needs for the wedding did not always align with theirs. And I felt, like, "I'm the bride, so just listen to me and nobody else!" He felt caught in the middle of it all, and I was his anxiety receptacle. I might as well have worn a sign around my neck that said, "Dump Neuroses Here." Then he told me I was reckless with money. I told him he needed a better job . . .

This fight lasted forty-eight hours, and I thought it would lead to a full cancellation of the wedding. However, one of the two nights during the argument, we had plans to meet my newly dumped cousin Mitch for BBQ, which forced us to make nice, and ultimately forced us to remember that we're a couple getting married in two weeks, who had sauce all over their faces. It's hard to stay angry when you both look like sloppy toddlers.

I don't know that there's a big lesson here. Stress was upon us, we fought, and it dissipated. Maybe I need to make room for that idea: In our marriage, stress may cause fights, and those fights won't kill us. Did they make us stronger? Not really. But maybe not every fight needs to be transformative and full of teaching moments.

WAYS TO SQUISH YOUR DOUBTS ABOUT MARRIAGE:

- Ask your close married friends what they fight about most. If they say we don't fight, get new friends because that's annoying. Or, brace yourself; they will divorce soon.

- Realize that no matter whom you date, you will grow to see his or her flaws, complexities, and psychological nooks and crannies. This doesn't end when you meet a new person. It just resets to zero, and then eventually you see the same number of flaws in that person as well. Maybe the flaws are different, but they are the same, quantity-wise.

- Stop watching sitcoms: They make American marriage look so depressing. Nagging wife, pushover dad, asshole kids. Hilarious! That does not and will not be you and your husband if you get those influences as far away from you as possible.

But reader beware: Brides are at risk for a plethora of other health issues. Until *WebMD Bridal* becomes an actual thing, I'm here to walk you through the potential health hazards that you should be aware of. Hypochondriacs, rejoice!

Generalized Nuptial Anxiety Disorder. The most common affliction contracted during the Wedding Planning Process. After reading bridal mags and wedding blogs, and consulting with friends and planning professionals, the bride-to-be is so caught up in every detail that she is convinced that the world will be destroyed if the wrong flatware is used when the salad course is served. There is also extra meaning and symbolism read into every detail of the ceremony and reception.

Advicitis. Anxiety and sickness caused by the terrible marriage advice you are constantly receiving. It will mostly come from the miserable people who believe there is honor in sticking by a mistake until they die. Many years of happy marriage lead you to keep your mouth shut because there's no advice to give: You either did it or you didn't. The unhappily married will make you ill with their marriage tips. It usually involves listening to what you're told and turning a blind eye to possible infidelity. You will want to lie down in the road at the thought of being Kate Winslet in *Revolutionary Road*. If you haven't seen the movie yet, wait until you've been married a few years and are in a good place.

Destiny Dysentery. Intense (you guessed it) diarrhea caused by a combination of stress and the juice cleanse you decided to go on because you want to get down to a dress size that makes your bridal party hate your guts. The toilet will be your best friend throughout this process. So much so that you should probably appoint it maid of honor. You will be running off to the bathroom so much that loved ones will think you have a cocaine problem. That is probably less embarrassing than to break the news to them that you have the squirts, so let them think it. Nobody will have the balls to stage an intervention until after the wedding, and then you can tell everyone that you kicked the habit, and everyone will congratulate you on your strength.

Sudden Adult-Onset ADHD . . . or At Least That's How You'll Try to Pass It Off to Co-Workers Who Don't Know What That Really Looks Like. The constant barrage of questions and problems that come up will absolutely make its way into your professional life in a way that will at first charm your co-workers and eventually piss off your boss. It will have you texting during a meeting (a meeting that could have been an e-mail anyway) and yelling into your iPhone in that hallway that everybody uses for angry phone calls. Your work will suffer in a way that hasn't happened since you were first out of college and had a problem with the vodka/work-life balance. Even when someone is talking to you about something very important, you can't hear a word because you are making seating charts in your head. When your direct supervisor is telling you that you need to get some overdue time sheets in by noon, all you're hearing is your aunt Barbara complaining that she has to sit next to the nephew that got mega sauced at your brother's wedding and called her the C word. Well, Barb, that's called family. P.S. The nephew claims he called her a "runt."

Honey's Simplex. Much worse than the easily hidden genital herpes, stress-induced cold sores around your mouth are very public and make the bride look like she went on one last crazy run in Vegas and now her poor husband has to marry damaged goods.

Ebol-in-Law. In some cases, the mother of the groom is a flesh-eating virus. In particular, those who didn't have good enough eggs to produce a baby girl. They have opinions based on what they did forty years ago, but guess what, Fairy Groomsmother, we don't throw rice anymore because it wastes food and I'm pretty sure it kills birds. It's enough to make you sick to your stomach, and it will. You'll feel like you are going to die. The only hope is to quarantine yourself until the symptoms die down.

Placating Identity Disorder. Going from your parents to his parents to the flower guy to the cake sisters to the venue woman who is never available so you have to talk to her dim bulb of an assistant, you are constantly changing who you are because this one's offended by curse words, and if you don't say "no lilies" fifty times, your reception will look like a funeral. But if you try to tell the baking "genius" that you want chocolate ganache more than once, they will be insulted and cancel the whole thing.

Cure-All. The only known cure for these ailments is to get a slight buzz on and stop giving a shit.

PERSPECTIVE? *getting some*

ONE WAY TO DEFLATE PANIC IS TO STOP CALLING YOUR wedding your "Big Day." Every book or site that casually uses that phrase ("How to Stop Climate Change . . . from Ruining Your Big Day!") wants you to believe that the day you get hitched is the biggest day of your life, all so they can sell you more items and services. Now, you might be really excited to buy a bunch of goods and services and are not looking for any reasons to stop. Nonetheless, letting go of the phrase "Big Day" can still have a positive effect.

Draw up a list of other Big Days you can look forward to in your life and gain a sense of perspective. They don't have to be Big Days in the eyes of the public, but days that will matter to you personally. If you can't think of any such days after five minutes, or thirty seconds, do not skip the exercise. In order to enjoy your wedding and planning it, and avoid being the woman who tries to slap a bird (one of the white doves you "hired") because the photo booth lacks prop diversity—feather boas galore, nary a mustache glued to a kebab skewer in sight—you'll need this perspective.

OTHER "BIG DAYS" TO LOOK FORWARD TO

- Your twenty-fifth high school reunion (I'd like to arrive at mine by private jet).

- The birth of a kid or five.

- Any brunch of any kind, big or small.

- Strolling around SoHo on a sunny day and buying cheap jewelry from some artist who doesn't know his own value.

- The day you impulse-buy a Chanel bag. (It is like shopper's heroin. You experience a huge high, followed by a huge low, and you don't even have to go to Skid Row! You just have to drop three months' rent irresponsibly! Post-purchase, yes, you will experience a tidal wave of guilt. Not just buyer's remorse, but full-on, materialistic postpartum. You shun the bag. You hide it in your closet. But then, months later, when your bitchy rich friend's wedding comes up, you go, "Hey! I have the bag for that!" And out comes the exquisite little bastard that will passive-aggressively shame everyone.)

- Getting carded at a bar. (My mom was recently carded at a Mexican restaurant and it made her year. She is sixty-one. Killing it. *Muy caliente*.)

- Driving down Highway 1. (There is nothing like it. Gorgeous views. Photo ops galore. Makes you feel like you're on a spiritual journey even if you're mostly doing it for the Instagram likes.)

- Doing mushrooms.

- The day your father finally admits he loves romantic comedies more than *The Godfather*. (My dad legitimately loved *Sweet November* and will always go with me to see chick flicks. My own mother won't even go. My dad is essentially my straight gay best friend.)

- The day you had a not-terrible-tasting, gluten-free pastry and genuinely thought it had wheat in it. Less glamorous, but thrilling nonetheless and, hey, it could happen.

BIG DAYS THAT ARE HISTORICAL AND YOU REALLY HOPE HAPPEN

The day someone cures cancer

The day Dan and I orgasm simultaneously

The day we learn the truth about JonBenét

BIG DAYS YOU CAN COUNT ON HAPPENING A NUMBER OF TIMES

Victoria's Secret annual sale—panties for three dollars, even the fancy ones

Christmas, loads of 'em!

Epic season finales

ALTERNATE WAYS TO REFER TO THE BIG DAY:

"that party" (the lack of capital letters gives it even less power)

Your Medium Day

Picture day

Day 1 out of 23,725 (based on sixty-five-year marriage)

Our zero'th anniversary

That thing

June 29 (insert your own date)

Seeing senior citizens in formal wear

Dances with dads (versus wolves)

Smooch judgment day

"Pressure to have sex tonight even though you just agreed to have sex with only each other for the rest of your lives, which really gets you in the mood" day

BLENDING FAMILIES INTO A PEOPLE SMOOTHIE
(no blades necessary)

I THINK THIS IS THE LARGEST GROWING PAIN OF ALL, BUT nobody really talks about it. The parents of your significant other, whom you might know well, or not well at all, are jumping to the next level of importance in your life. Their rank is changing. Add *your* parents into the mix, and their upgraded relationship with *your* partner. Then stir both sets of parents in together and see things *really* get interesting. "Why can't everybody just get along? We're all adults!" Great question. Let's explore it.

BIG BRIDAL: **Utilize traditions from both sides to add zest to your wedding.**

I SAY: **No, Big Bridal, I'm not talking about representing cultures through aesthetic details at the wedding. I'm talking about taking on strangers as FAMILY.**

A lot of people said, "Family will get involved. It can get ugly." I didn't think this would happen to me, and it did. Everyone was a monster claiming he or she wasn't a monster—Dan and me included.

It's as if Dan and I were around a boardroom table, as if we were about to settle a divorce out of court, only we weren't getting divorced, we were getting the opposite of divorced, we were getting married . . . But we'd forgotten how to love each other and be decent to each other because of wedding stress and families and whatnot . . . and for some fucked-up reason, instead of hiring lawyers as you would in a settlement to explain ourselves to one another, we'd hired our own parents. Actually, they'd hired themselves. We never asked. Dan's mom and dad in his corner, my mom and dad in mine. And even though we'd lived on our own and made plenty of decisions without our parents for years . . . suddenly we were regressing and consulting these unqualified "lawyers" to make sure they were happy because their happiness is our happiness? It's exactly what you don't want in a marriage: Too much outside input. Yet how Dan's parents felt mattered more than how I felt, and how I was upset made my mom upset and her discomfort made Dan upset because he wanted to maintain a good relationship with my mom. It was a mess.

My parents first met Dan's parents when they attended my grand-mother's funeral and shiva. I found out my grandma had passed away while I was staying with Charlene and Lenny. I had gone to New York to film *GirlCode* on a Friday and took the train to Long Island for a visit on Saturday. In the middle of the night, Charlene woke me up, handed me a cordless phone and I knew the news was going to be awful. It was my aunt Becky, hysterical, frazzled, sobbing, and screaming, "Do not leave New York. The funeral is this week. Don't go back to LA." Charlene and Lenny let me crawl into their bed and they pet my head while I cried. The next day, Charlene made me breakfast and brought me to Nordstrom Rack to shop for a funeral dress. She took me in like I was her daughter. It made the otherwise dreary experience as warm and comfortable as it could have been. I thought to myself, "When Dan and I get married, I have nothing to worry about. These people are the best family anyone could ask for."

At the shiva my parents and Dan's parents instantly bonded. I walked past my dad and Charlene discussing being school teachers over bagels. I remember my aunt Becky talking to Lenny. I remember Aunt Dana and Charlene chatting. I don't know what those conversations were about, but I remember making my way through the sadness party thinking, "Oh, everyone is merging so seamlessly. I'm lucky." I don't know what I expected. What was going to happen? Was Charlene going to climb on the table and dance the Macarena while everyone gasped in horror? Of course it went well. Because everyone was there for my grandma, and in turn, for my family. It wasn't about Dan's family getting along with the Lees. That was a subconcern of my own.

The first instance I felt tension was upon our engagement. Charlene called my mom, and my mom did not respond right away. That's because my mom is not a "phone person," and sometimes she's not even a text person or e-mail person. She kind of just waits to see you IRL to do a proper catch-up. Plus, she is anti-tradition, so it likely didn't occur to her to reach out to Charlene. She would reach out if it was her birthday, because she understands those more than engagements. (My mom never really had one.) So the moms were already a little out of sync. Then, there was discussion of the wedding being in either Dallas or New York. My parents pushed for Dallas, Dan's parents pushed for New York. The tug-o-war began . . .

When the wedding was set to be on Long Island, I felt pressure from my family-in-law to use vendors they recommended, friends of theirs, but my parents were in the camp of "Use whomever you jive with." When the wedding moved to Simi Valley, I felt bullied by Dan to have the wedding be more traditionally Jewish than I would have liked, and Dan felt frustrated because he deemed certain traditions nonnegotiable. Then, I overheard Dan's parents make a comment about my parents. Something to the effect of "They only have one kid. They should contribute more." Yep.

Whatever Dan's parents wanted, Dan wanted, and whatever I wanted, my parents wanted. I would often say to Dan, "Wait, are you the bride?!" Because that's how it felt. We were at war, a secret war that nobody was actively acknowledging. Dan and I did the battling, but Dan's parents fought me through him, and my parents stoked my fire by agreeing with whatever I was feeling. Although I have recovered (mostly) because the dust did settle post-wedding, I am not sure that our families love each other. Maybe one day they will, but are they an immediate match made in heaven? Uh . . .

I used to think that nobody disliked my family. I realize that sounds loco, but that was my experience growing up. My friends, friends of friends, boyfriends . . . I never hesitated to introduce them to my parents. I knew it would be easy because my parents are kind and laid-back. They use bad words, and you can use bad words in front of them. Fun! So Dan or his family talking any level of shit about them was brand new to me. (I never heard the shit-talking, except for that only-child comment, but I felt like it was happening. That was my hunch.)

Much less shocking, I would call my mom constantly, and vent about my experience. She would validate how I was feeling, obvs, because she's my mom. They're programmed to take your side. Plus, it is always easy to point fingers. It's the most convenient catharsis, to analyze how other people are fucked up versus looking within yourself. But Charlene and I were talking all the time, too! I enjoyed our conversations during this time, about the wedding, work, life. We were "close," sure, but I wasn't allowing myself to be *close* close. I didn't have the balls (er, the ovaries?) to truly voice how I felt about everything with Dan and the wedding, mostly because I didn't want to disappoint her or appear difficult. But here's the thing about appearing difficult: You can't control somebody's perception of you. So you might as well just say your difficult ideas, difficult bride, if that is you. There is no use concealing that side of you! Take it from someone who is difficult. Okay, I still don't *think* I'm difficult, but I know at least five people who would disagree immediately upon reading that, so maybe I am. The only thing worse than being difficult is being difficult but masquerading as easy, breezy, beautiful Bridal Girl.

We did a girls' trip to New York for dress shopping early on in my engagement, with my mom and aunts, Charlene and sis-in-law Emily, and my pal Jacqueline, and when we were all at Monique Lhuillier, I tried on a very pretty formfitting dress. When I stepped out of the dressing room, Emily said, "It makes you look fat." Or maybe she said heavy? Whatever it was, my mom whipped around and snapped, "She does not look heavy! Are you crazy?" It was the first sign of my mom and Dan's family not blending. Or is confrontation a sign of blending? There is a level of comfort required to even consider confrontation, so maybe it was a good sign? I just remember tensing up and scurrying back to the dressing room, overcome with anxiety.

Why is it so hard for the couple's parents to get along? Two things: jealousy and fear. Somebody is trying to infiltrate our nest (Fear!) and they might be better than us? (Jealousy!) Of course it's not a contest, but somehow it becomes one. Maybe they're preparing for when grandkids enter the picture and the real competition begins. *Which set of grandparents gets to see the little ones more? Where will Jamie and Dan prefer to spend their holidays? Will they favor one family over the other?* There's a lack of abundance mentality, like the kind people seem to possess when having children: "There's enough love to go around, whether we have one kid or eight kids," people say. With inherited family, parents slip into scarcity mode, terrified that we, the couple, will only be able to ration a certain amount of love and respect and time to the parties involved.

When I was growing up, my mom's parents were my *real* grandparents, which was sad for my dad. His mom was smart, sweet, and attentive, but she died when I was four, and his dad, was, well, a weirdo. Wealthy dude, divorced my grandmother when he decided to marry his (much younger) secretary—split his time between Arizona, Idaho, and France. He never came to visit us because my step-grandmother, Bess, would not fly on airplanes. Not out of fear, but because she couldn't smoke on planes. So "visiting my grandparents" on my dad's side meant taking a trip to Tucson, Arizona, spending all day bored either going to the one museum there or driving to the one, somewhat cool, strip in downtown with the one, somewhat cool, vintage store. We wouldn't see my grandfather until dinnertime, when we would meet him at his country club. Also, we never stayed with my grandfather and Bess at their house, and they had plenty of room. It was a very surface relationship. My mom's parents, on the other hand, called frequently and visited Dallas every chance they got. And we visited them every chance we got. It was great.

The competitive spirit is alive in Dan's family, too. Drawing comparisons between his mom and Emily's mom, Dan will assess who's the "better grandma" to Dan's nephews, even though both grandmothers live nearby and see the boys on a regular basis. "Why is it a contest?" I ask. Dan replies, "It's not." And then we change the subject.

I call this the Competitive Grandparenting Phenomenon™. I suspect that on some level, parents absorb these experiences with their own parents, and then when their kids get engaged they start vying for the role of "best grandparents." This dynamic is so powerful it's on full display even though Dan and I don't have children yet. It's a conscious, or subconscious—I haven't decided—pleading for the spot in the yet-to-be-born child's memory of "Who loves me more?" Because, apparently, there can only be one winner! And it is usually the mom's side of the family who wins.

So now you have more clarity on *why* blending can be so charged, but the question remains: What can you do? One option? Throw a *Mom Shower,* which is like a bridal shower, but for moms, because they seem to have a real need to feel seen and heard during the WPP. Have a separate party honoring them, and then maybe the attention can be successfully refocused back on the bride for the rest of the engagement? I'm kidding, but if you can work it into your budget, I'm not kidding.

But in all seriousness, you can't control people getting along. It will happen or it won't happen. I realized that a lot of my anxiety was self-generated. I suffer from people-pleasing, fear of confrontation, fear that confrontation is a sign that "things are bad," and it's not. It can be a sign of people working it out, making it better, making it stronger.

The days leading up to my wedding, all I could think about, in addition to "Ooo, my pants feel big," was "I hope everybody gets along." I didn't think a fight would break out. Worse. I feared that people would be internally fuming. I wouldn't see signs. They would just be secretly brooding, and there would be nothing tangible for me to point to to fix. It was maddening. The Friday morning before my wedding, I walked to Gelson's with my dad and Charlene to show my dad what snacks I would have him buy for the bridal party. He was up ahead of Charlene and me, and she turned to me and said, "Your parents are adorable. I don't know what you were talking about!" I have no recollection of saying they weren't adorable, but whatever—I was thrilled to hear this. It put me at such ease. It was the validation I needed to chill the fuck out.

I vow to accept that only time can successfully blend two families.

BACH, please

PERHAPS THIS IS A GOOD TIME TO TAKE A BREAK FROM THE drama . . . and plan another event! Ditch the family dynamics, grab some friends (and their dynamics), and go celebrate.

> **BIG BRIDAL SAYS:** Fourteen Bachelorette Themes! Including a spa day . . .
>
> **I SAY:** No matter how you class it up, the theme of every bachelorette event is "Basic Bitch," so you might as well go with the old standbys of liquor and lap dances.

I had my bachelorette party in Vegas, and I, with the help of Bonnie and Erin, planned it. However, my guilt crept up so I could never fully say, "Take over the majority of the scheduling. I'm promoting you to co-chairwomen of Lady Debauchery, Inc.!" I wanted to be CHILL BRIDE. And chill bride plans her own festivities so as not to burden her friends.

I e-mailed the bachelorette crew, about thirteen girls, about how I had found a good deal for a block of rooms at MGM Grand. Everyone wrote back, "Great!" "Cool!" "I'm already drunk!" Before reserving the rooms,

I realized that The Mirage had a better pool, and was only four dollars more, so I booked Mirage. Everyone wrote back, co-signing. A few hours later, DBF (Distant Best Friend) says, "I can't stay at The Mirage. Morally, I don't feel right about staying in a hotel with tigers in captivity. I'm going to stay across the street."

I was smacked with disbelief, because I don't actively think about the well-being of any animals other than Dennis and Dan. But I'm a good person, I swear! I tried to sway DBF. "The tigers are not inside the hotel. They're not casually strolling about the casino sniping mozz sticks from blackjack tables. They're in a separate attraction in the back of the hotel." It didn't matter. She didn't want to be in a hotel that supported caged kitties. "What about girls in cages, suspended from the ceiling of Tao, dancing to put themselves through dental college?" "Those matter less because they're not furry." "Good point."

If Bonnie or Erin had been in charge of handling Tigergate 2016, all I would have heard is "DBF will be staying across the street. She has points with that hotel that she needs to use to help pay for the trip." "Cool. Now let's talk strippers."

Learn from my mistakes with these simple tips:

- If you're doing a bachelorette party, I'd say have someone else plan it. Otherwise, brace yourself for "wrenches," friends with plans that don't align with yours. (For the record, I have been a wrench many times, and am happy to head up Wrenches Anonymous.)

- If you go to Vegas, choose the best hotel you can and just hang out there the whole time. Nightclub, restaurants, shows, pools . . . all no more than an elevator ride away. It's when you start making plans at other hotels that everything gets complicated. You start walking as a group down the strip, one person's feet start to hurt, next thing you know that person and four others have gone back to the hotel for the night.

- Embrace the tacky. Ultimately the cheesy stuff paid off, if in unexpected ways. Most of the lap dances my friends and I got were 99 percent funny and 1 percent sexy. Which is a decent ratio. The guys wore a ton of cologne, greased their abs, and ripped off tear-away track pants to reveal Lycra bike shorts. Funny. But this one guy straddled me and was super sweaty, to the point where I could smell his *scent*—a hint of B.O.—unmasked by seventeen layers of Cool Water like the rest of the gang. It was TMI. I just met you, man. I don't need to know what you smell like when you get out of Barry's Bootcamp.

- Dick hats, silly as they may be, serve a purpose. I don't understand how this tradition originated . . . Straight guys love "catchin' puss" (sorry), but you've never seen a bachelor party wearing labia fedoras, drinking out of clit straws. Still, ultimately I'm for it because it lets strangers know whom to shower with attention and free drinks.

 *I vow to allow someone else to be the planner and to embrace accessorizing with genitalia.*

Dress, Hair,
and Makeup

WEDDING DIET:
lose to gain

PUPPETEERING YOUR WEIGHT BEFORE YOUR WEDDING CAN TAKE on many forms—skipping meals or avoiding carbs or working out with a militant personal trainer who says things like, "We gotta fix those birthing hips because you ain't even had kids yet." (Direct quote from the one personal trainer I had in my life.) This is undeniably crazy, but unlike many other elements of the wedding, your weight is something you can kind of manage.

> **BIG BRIDAL SAYS:** Here's a healthy and effective six-month plan to get that wedding-ready physique!
>
> **I SAY:** You will probably lose everything you wanted to lose in under a month from stress and excitement alone. This is not healthy or FDA-approved, but in terms of cold hard numbers, the adrenaline diet is extremely effective.

This is where I tell you, "Do not lose an ounce. Girls who get too skinny for their wedding look scary." I, of course, believe this, but I also feel bangin' when I'm at my thinnest. I want to be rational and body-positive and progressive. But I am also a human woman, and when I envisioned my wedding day, I wanted to look like my hottest possible self.

I am the first to admit that this is twisted and weirdly psychological, but to me, with Wedding Weight Control, there is an element of punishment that feels naughty, but thrilling. It's terrible. It's sad. It's riveting. It's like cutting, except replace flesh with calories. If you *don't* lose weight for your wedding, you are a star, a treasure, and I love you for it. But if you are like me, a loon who somehow reverted back to the early '90s where "fitness" was taking walks and starving yourself, you're going to want to read on. Let's have an open discussion here. This is an acknowledgment of the psychosis that is wedding dieting.

If you can commit to starting a fitness/nutrition routine anywhere between six months and three months before the wedding, there is a chance you won't gain back as much weight after the wedding. But you are going to gain some back. And if you're like me, you will gain it all back on your honeymoon in Cabo, where you drank three four-hundred-calorie piña coladas before ten A.M. daily. Maybe you think I'm about to say, "Considering the fact that you'll gain it back, why diet in the first place?" I know what I'm about to say is truly sad and disgusting to admit, but . . . I love looking back on my wedding and thinking, "Not only was it fun, but I was thin." It's another layer of happiness. (Ugh, I can't believe I just typed that.)

What is so special about being thinner at your wedding? It's not like I was trying to lose weight for graduation day or for my first job (I mean, I definitely did for my first breakup). But you see what I'm getting at. Why is a wedding the skinny milestone? I think it's for two reasons:

- A wedding is a pageant. There's no swimsuit competition, but I definitely waved and smiled with teeth so bright white, they were almost blue, and my skintight dress was easily as restrictive as a Lycra two-piece.

- It's the most photographed milestone. You will take a lot of pictures when you have your first kid, but if you are wearing a ton of makeup in those hospital pics, you'll look like a self-involved nightmare. The kid will grow up to look back at those pictures and think, "Uh, it wasn't about you, lady."

I vow to weigh whatever I weigh on my wedding day, whether that weight is the product of the healthiest of dieting regimes, a profound self-acceptance, or the weight-loss plan of all wealthy white women who came before me: Mild starvation, control issues, and severe mental and emotional stress brought on by unachievable expectations.

For someone determined to be a Skinny Bitch™ and go hard with my weight-loss goals right before the wedding, I was put in some pretty challenging situations: I ate, a lot, at my job. Up until two weeks before my wedding, I was in a writer's room for an HBO show with breakfast, lunch, and sometimes dinner brought in from the best restaurants on the west side of Los Angeles. As far as day jobs go, it was a piglet's paradise. It's not even like an NYC writing gig, where in theory you could insist on walking a block to a restaurant to get your lunch. The culture is "Don't move. Just eat."

I would wake up every morning, drive the one-hour commute to Santa Monica, arrive at my job, and my breakfast order would be there: Scrambled eggs, four huge slices of bacon, a side of avocado, and a cup of mango. And two biscuits. With butter and homemade jam. I would be stuffed, but because of the nature of a writer's room, if you aren't thinking about jokes, you are taking your "hunger temperature": Checking in with yourself to see if you are slightly hungry, somewhat hungry, or severely hungry.

"What about *not* hungry?" I believe that there is no such thing as "not hungry" at any job that forces you to sit all day. You are always 10 percent hungry because you are always at least 10 percent bored. Well, really, you are always 10 percent bored, just in life. But when you are sitting all day, the subtle rise and fall of your emotions, your micro-moods, are just more palpable. You are hyper in touch with yourself.

I would chow down on breakfast, and before I even took my last bite of offensively huge bacon, I would be passed the menu for lunch to place that order. I was still digesting breakfast, and they were already shoving soup and sandwich options at us.

This was, in theory, a luxurious job perk, constant nourishment, never needing to ever ask "Is anyone else hungry?" But I experienced it as the seventh circle of hell . . . a den of temptation I was being paid to show up to right while I was in the midst of a mission: To take wedding pictures that I would look back on and not just think "Wow, that was special," but "Wow, I had a Kelly Ripa bod."

It was time to bring in digital support. I began using a calorie-counting app called LoseIt! (which is ironic because I was *losing it,* mentally) the August before my wedding but would use it like an idiot. It tracks your progress weekly, resetting your allotment of calories on Mondays, so on Sunday night, when I would be on the road for stand-up, bored and alone in a hotel room in Tempe, Arizona, I would eat a piece of carrot cake, and then deduct five hundred calories from the next day, and I would repeat this cycle for weeks, and my weight stayed consistent. Because I don't know if you know this, but weight loss does not involve scarfing down cake? Crazy! I know!

So needless to say I was not losing weight as I had hoped—slow and steady, the healthy way.

Between August and February, six months on a weight-loss app, I had lost, count it, ONE POUND. And I had nine and a half more to go to get to my goal weight of 118.

Where did I come up with a number so specific and random as 118? I'll tell you: My average weight when I was a freshman in HS, when I felt like my body was at its peak hotness, was 123. The summer before sophomore year, I went on the SlimFast diet, drinking two shakes a day and eating Kraft Mac & Cheese as my third meal, just incredibly balanced nutrition, and I got down to 115. I felt immaculate: Hot in a swimsuit, just a shell of perfection.

Since it feels slightly unreasonable to have the *exact* body I had as an early high schooler, only a few years older than a straight-up tween, I figured, "Let's add three pounds because of bone density or whatever. Aging weight." Because that makes SO much sense. (Please note sarcasm and self-hatred.)

That's how I reached 118.

Listening to an average-weight girl hootin' and hollerin' about her size leading up to her wedding, you might be thinking things like: (a) Who cares? (b) Do you have an eating disorder? (c) This is exactly what the patriarchy wants women to worry about, and you can't be a victim to that kind of contrived pressure. (d) But seriously, are you this shallow?

a. I do.

b. Maybe? Also: Who doesn't? Varying levels exist, and I am not here to minimize those who suffer with much greater severity than I ever have. But if you are a woman living in America with no food issues, you are a heroine.

c. I know. I hate it with every part of my being, yet I'm not above it . . . yet.

d. Yes.

The upside to dieting, aside from the way you'll look, is that it distracts you from all of the noise of wedding planning. It becomes a fun, but stupid game, so stupid that you're not even rewarded with a cash prize, you're rewarded with clothes feeling loose and your husband telling you, "You need to eat."

The funniest moment in the Wedding Weight-loss Journey, the WWJ (which Dan would probably love because it sounds like WWE), was when Dan's friend, Jon, was in town from San Diego, about a month before the Medium Day (see "Perspective," page 193). We took him to our favorite BBQ place, which has two menus you can order from: the BBQ one, and one for this other restaurant that operates out of the same kitchen with salads, pastas, etc. Dan and I ordered ribs and a side of creamy Brussels sprouts, excited for Jon to also order BBQ. But, no, he goes for the salad menu. Big mistake. A Caesar with chicken? What is this, Chili's Too at the airport? That is such a hellacious choice. But, whatever, he's an adult, let him live his life. Anyway, this poses a subtle threat to Dan, who is trying to get fit for the wedding. He's been working out a lot, eating pretty paleo, mostly meat and vegetables. It also sent me into a panic: "Should we all order salads? We are only a month out. Jon isn't even getting married, and he is eating like a bride."

Jon's response to me? "I like that you aren't losing a bunch of weight like most brides."

How dare he?! I had lost four pounds since joining the app and intended to lose six more. Am I going to eat a salad for dinner? No. Am I going to make any sacrifices or remotely modify my menu selection? No. Is that what dieting is, though? Yes. FUCK!

Then Charlene called me one day saying, "I reached my goal weight for the wedding!" I couldn't let her win. I had to reach mine, too. I also said I wasn't going to eat carbs the month before the wedding and then found myself eating pancakes multiple times. Fuck diets.

In the end, the only diet that worked for me was the Stressed into Skinny diet:

Are you in a great relationship with someone who loves you for you? Sounds like a recipe for FAT! If you want to really shed the pounds, it's not about nutritionally depriving yourself, it's about confronting the fact that you're about to dive into your new life with an anxious Jewish man who keeps declaring that the wedding is "ruining his life." You might just stop eating! I did.

Stressed to Skinny! There's no such thing as hunger when you're being yelled at about how the red flowers on the chuppah look too much like a Christmas wreath!

This really is how I lost weight. It's the nasty truth, but it is the truth nonetheless. Between errands, last-minute tasks, arranging and rearranging seating charts, my own personal beauty maintenance (waxing, plucking, haircutting, etc.) and nonstop, blow-out, record-scratching fights with Dan, I just dropped the pounds. I didn't hit 118, but I hit 120, and that was close enough.

To my beautiful bride-to-be: If you're stressed about getting that "wedding bod," just know that that is yet another source of anxiety that Big Bridal adds to your list. Also know that you're not alone and that I was a full-fledged member of the club. I wanted to lose weight for my wedding because of all the bullshit reasons that we all want to lose weight for our weddings: Every person I know would be there (at least it felt like it); I paid a ton of money for the photographer (and my future children would one day see the pictures and say, "Daaaaayum, Mom was a total babe"); white is a truly unforgiving color; I wanted my guests to literally see my commitment to my body as a metaphor for my commitment to this relationship . . . But then it all went to shit because I am a real person with a real job and life and so even though I had every intention of getting sucked into calorie counting and aggressive workouts, I simply didn't have the means to make it work. On the flip side, I ended up losing weight from the unsurmountable stress. Winning!

DRESSES
and excesses

THIS PART IS SO FUN. I'M OBSESSED WITH WEDDING DRESSES, wedding dress shopping, wedding dress altering, being in a bridal shop and seeing what other people are trying on, and how their taste differs from mine. You can stress about every other aspect of the wedding, but don't stress about what is essentially a magnificent costume. It's even less difficult than finding a costume because, when you're assembling a costume, you go to five stores looking for the perfect Bill Clinton mask. When you're searching for a dress, you will try on *so* many viable options. Just don't buy anything until you absolutely love it, because you can't return that shit.

BIG BRIDAL SAYS: **Find something classic, not trendy.**

I SAY: **Find something you feel gorgeous in. If that means a weird white ceremonial robe with feathers stuck to it, by God, wear it, you regal chicken.**

Classic usually means 1950s and '60s Hollywood glam. That seems pretty kitschy to me. Audrey Hepburn? She had a beehive, which is hardly a current look. When you look back at your wedding photos thirty years from now, you're not going to say, "I can't believe I wore that! Lace is so tacky now." You're going to say, "Wow, look at how much more collagen I had in my skin." Youthful skin is a powerful, timeless outfit. And you are wearing your skin on your wedding day! Hopefully your own and not someone else's? (Serial killer much?) Even if you get married at seventy, when you're ninety, you'll look through the wedding album thinking, "Ahhh, my youth." Unless you are a superhuman Anna Wintour 2.0 who can laser-peer into the future and predict trends in the year 2060, relax. What you wear at your wedding will someday be out of date. It is truly impossible to avoid. So whatever fashion is of the moment, enjoy it, embrace it, rock it.

The dress is, hands down, the thing I cared about most when I got engaged. I wanted it more than I wanted a wedding. I was, like, "Can I just get a gown, and casually wear it while I'm perusing the salad bar at Whole Foods?" The week I got engaged, I applied through TLC.com to be on *Say Yes to the Dress,* and I got on the show! Well, eventually I got on. It wasn't immediate. And on camera I did say "yes," but that is not the actual wedding dress I wore. Did I lie on television?! Sort of, but I can explain!

I had already bought my dress at Neiman's when I went to Dallas to visit my mom. I got so swept up in shopping in my hometown, very nostalgic, that I purchased the dress while I was wearing it, in *Say Yes to the Dress* fashion. (Note: *Say Yes to the Dress* is a somewhat socially irresponsible show because it makes brides crave that moment of "This is it! Stop everything! I found it!" as opposed to loving the dress but allowing yourself to keep looking just to be sure.) Anyway, at this time, I had not heard back from the show, so I assumed, "Whatever. Guess I won't be going to Kleinfeld in New York. Doesn't hurt that I bought my dress."

Two days later, guess who comes knocking on my door (sending me a brief, detached e-mail)? *Say Yes to the Dress*! The first question they asked me, "Did you already buy your dress?" I lied. I said no. I know it was wrong, but I wanted to be on the show so bad, I would do whatever it took to get on it. So the new plan was: Go on the show with my hilarious comedian friends Phoebe Robinson and Jacqueline Novak, while knowing in advance that I was going to have the "I can't decide" storyline and just be the girl who never bought anything. Better than not going on the show at all, right? Not quite. They are looking to make a sale, so when you go on without buying something, you are a real pain-in-the-ass thorn in their side. "Wait, they don't buy you your dress when you go on the show?" Oh, hell no. I wish.

This is where it gets messy. At the shoot, I tried on this gorgeous Dennis Basso dress, which truly made me doubt the dress I had purchased. So my thought in the "say yes" moment was "just say yes." Worry about the money later. Buy this one. You can sell the other one! So I said yes on TV, but after we finished filming, I fell back down to Earth like Nicolas Cage in *City of Angels* (aww, I miss '90s Meg Ryan), and realized that having two dresses that look virtually identical is insane. And the one from Neiman's was free . . . because my aunt bought it for me. I had truly gone insane. I was a Bridopath. I remember when we were filming, and I said yes, staring into the floor-length mirror, I locked eyes with Jacqueline who was behind me mouthing, "What are you doing?!" I didn't know what I was doing. And THAT is the power of wedding dress shopping. You get swept away, caught up in the magic. It is the closest to being on a cloud—if clouds contained a committee of friends and family having visceral reactions to you in clothing.

I recommend that you go in knowing that it's likely not going to be a snap decision where you start crying and screaming, "This is it!!!" . . . where a panel of friends, family, store employees, other moms in the store and their daughters, the homeless man outside who caught a glimpse of you through the window and dropped his trash sandwich in awe, all clap and cheer as you twirl beneath a shower of snow like Winona Ryder in *Edward Scissorhands*.

Also, don't expect people to cry when you walk out of the dressing room. Nobody in my family did. My friends, my mom, myself, nobody. The reaction was more "How much is this one?"

Currency Exchange: Wedding Gowns

Five thousand dollars, what my dress cost, is a lot of money. It doesn't sound like what a rational, modern woman would spend on a dress to be worn one day. But in the wicked, warped world of wedding dresses, you gotta open your heart, mind, and wallet to $3K and over. And it's *okay* to read that "K" the way you would if it was texted to you by a passive-aggressive shitty friend. Because the price is shitty. But it's a reality. It's a disgusting racket, but a rrrreally pretty, fun one.

You can't make money appear out of thin air, but you caaan use puppy-dog eyes on your divorced aunt with no children to whom you're like a daughter . . . to see if she'll buy the dress of your dreams. Okay, I didn't use puppy-dog eyes on Becky, but she did offer to buy my wedding dress, unsolicited because she's like a second mom who will always feel 2 percent sorry for me from the days when I was a struggling comedian and couldn't afford my own rent. Initially, Becky thought this meant $2K max because when she got married, she got a dress that was white, but not bridal, at Neiman's that cost less than a grand. Whether you have a Becky or a Bank of America student checking account, just remove your sense of reality when it comes to dollar signs here.

Pricing Brackets

If you pull this off, you are a true badass. It is a sign of maturity, grace, and balanced priorities. You are not lazy and basic like me.

- Don't be fooled by online images. Try this stuff on in person, because up close you might see shit get weird when it comes to fabric . . . sometimes the whites are that REAL white, like a costume from *Frozen on Ice*, or the sequins have that pink tint, quinceañera-style, that wasn't visible online.

- Try BHLDN, Anthropologie's company. They have a range of beautiful options, in that price range . . . although there were a few too many hippie ones in the mix to let me trust them. I'm not a shoeless farm bride, and I don't want my dress rubbing up against any rustic dresses in the warehouse and getting commie ideas.

- Sift through the items at David's Bridal. There are gems in there, but David's not gonna make it easy.

- Find a gorgeous dress that isn't meant to be bridal, but totally can be if you have a vision and can handle not having the experience of going to a bridal store.

- Try cool brands that happen to have a few white options that they call their bridal collection, like Reformation.

- Watch out for princess ball gowns. I've noticed that when these cost less than a grand, they don't look great. Those gowns require a certain amount of material to be poufy, so do the math on fabric quality. You might need to readjust your vision if you are not willing to budge on style. Spend more OR get something in a different shape. Sheath dresses are reliable in this bracket.

$1–$3K

This pricing will get you into the standard fancy bridal shops, but depending on the shop, they'll try to upsell you. From my experience, the dresses I saw at Kleinfeld in this bracket (and I did try on a few . . . fourteen) look cheaper than they should, given the cost. I've seen beautiful dresses that cost in this bracket, but I noticed a distinct lack of them at ol' Kleiny-poos. And the problem with that is, it is TOO MUCH MONEY FOR THEM TO LOOK ANYTHING OTHER THAN DECADENT AND PERFECT. I think they purposely make not great choices on the lower price stock to inspire you to head back to the higher-price materials.

- Consider buying used. For this significant dough, you could get a high-end dress that was only worn once. "But what if the person who wore it before me got divorced? Will I be cursed?" Yes, so tell your MoH to perform a sage ritual on it before you wear it, NBD.

- Try your luck at a sample sale. I went with my friend to a Pronovias sample sale for her wedding, and while she found something, the dress still cost over $3K. And Pronovias is considered "reasonable" in the bridal world.

$3–$5K

Yes, this is where I found my dress. I wanted to go to a classic bridal atelier for that whole experience. I was willing to beg, borrow, or steal to make that happen.

- The quality of dresses above $3K will, as one would hope, impress you. No fabrics at this price evoke satin pajamas worn by the *Golden Girls*.

- It's a luxury bracket, and thus it affords you a certain experience. At this price, the sales people won't snarl at you for not going higher, but once you purchase, you will feel sick. Make sure garbage cans are nearby as the credit card swipes. For you or whoever is buying. And make sure you have a can of Sprite to drink like you just passed out from giving blood. Purchasing a wedding dress and doling out platelets in the back of a van? Similar symptoms.

$5–$7K

I considered heading into this realm, but I just couldn't do it even if I could have done it.

- Yes, your dress will be gorgeous. On the rack, on the floor, on your body upside down. It's sort of comforting when you see that something that costs that much does seem to be of better quality, but it doesn't mean something of lesser quality is bad quality! It's like additional coffee cup holders in a car— only you can tell me if they're of value to you.

- Dresses start to fit your body in a way you didn't even know they could. If you're an hourglass, you'll be so hourglass your fiancé will be stoked to turn ya over! Hey, hey, hey! Sorry. Seriously, if you're an apple, you're the apple that tempted Eve, Snow White, and that algebra teacher who's in jail now.

$7–$10K

I tried one that was $9K that I was obsessed with. My mom encouraged me to "just do it," and I "just couldn't." Even if I helped my aunt pay . . . Two people going in on a dress like we're co-investing in a racehorse? No. No, thanks. It's just too crazy. It's irresponsible. *If you can't afford this bracket, do not try on dresses within it.* I still dream about the one that costs $9K. Why? Where will I wear it? It was Pnina Tornai, too, and all her dresses have the trashiest elegance; you look like a sexy pirate. It's so silly and I love it.

- Your designer dress—it better be designer at that price— can be resold . . . but for how much? Hard to say. Are you interested in pursuing the dress market after your wedding? Something to point out: Having a designer wedding dress is not the same thing as having a designer handbag. Designer bags are fairly recognizable: The Celine one has those wings at the opening; Louis Vuitton has the signature print; the Birkin is square and dull, but for some reason coveted. They have a specific look that people can point to and go, "Wow, she is either rich, terrible with the little money she does earn, or ventured into the depths of China Town for the perfect fake." People are not going to recognize the designer who made your wedding gown. If you care who made it, great. But it will not elicit attention if that's what you're looking for.

- Is it really worth it? Very easy to get caught up in shifting your budget around to make the dress work. Make sure before you purchase that you try on the cheaper version of the same dress, just to make sure you can't live without it.

$10K AND UP

- I love you, you fucking psycho. No judgment. You're Beyoncé. Who judges Beyoncé? Only a monster.

Trying on is fun! Sure, seeing a bunch of options can be overwhelming, but if you remember that you only get to do this once, it will make you want to see what is out there. The stores are so fun. If you get easily overwhelmed, pick two stores tops and decide on something between the two. Or be like me, and keep shopping til you're about six months out . . . so you have enough time to order and alter.

If all this is making you pissed off about money, consider just getting a ten-dollar dress at H&M. Spend the money you were considering spending on a sponsorship or charity. Then, print the images of the dolphins you saved (or redwoods you planted) on the inside of your skirt. Throughout the evening, lift up the hem of your bargain dress and say, "This is where the dress money went." Also, consider cost of printing. You might want to just give that to charity, too.

Dress Styles: They All Have Pluses and Minuses

A wedding dress is personal, very personal for how physically superficial it is. Just know once again you can't go wrong. It's just a piece of clothing you put on your body to make yourself feel glamorous. Yes, guests will view and judge, but no matter what they really think, they'll tell you that you look perfect. Just get what you want because the compliments will be the same either way.

MERMAID

PROS:

- Looks great on everyone.
- Safe—like a Julianne Hough—just nice to look at and simple and harmless.
- The Little Mermaid was hot.

CONS:

- Everyone wears them.
- Is this a trend that we will look back on and think, what were we thinking?
- I hate sparkle belts, and a lot of mermaid dresses demand them; just the phrase "sparkle belt" . . . it's like if Elton John did karate.

TRUMPET

PROS:

- Like a mermaid, but with more structure.
- Trumpet is a cool instrument; puffy cheeks, jazz bands in the West Village, love it.

CON:

- Wait, jazz is actually kind of annoying.

BALL GOWN

PROS:

- Covers up your butt, thighs, legs; I'm pear shaped, so this sounds like a dream.

- Makes you feel like a princess.

- It feels the most bridal; you might wear a white dress again, but chances are you won't wear a white ball gown again.

CONS:

- Not great for the outdoors—always weird to wear a ball gown on grass.

- The princess thing is a little juvenile; Disney vibes aren't cute when you're thirty-two.

A WHITE(ISH?) DRESS THAT YOU JUST FIND SOMEWHERE (VINTAGE STORE, BACK OF A FRIEND'S CLOSET, SAMPLE SALE, WHATEVER)

PROS:

- You are so chill, and everyone will know it.

- This is very adult of you.

CON:

- Is it *that* cool to not give AF? This is your WEDDING. You don't need to be all emo about it.

YOUR GRANDMA'S OR MOM'S DRESS

PRO:

- Amazing tribute to an amazing woman.

- Amazing tribute to a shitty woman who had amazing taste.

CON:

- Poufy sleeves and a high neck make you look like you are posing for one of those sad haunting Victorian family portraits. When you see it on the wall in a museum, you're like, "Can we get the fuck out of this room? The eyes in that painting are following me."

Dan's Suit

My husband needed a new suit for the wedding, and so during a trip to his parents' house in Long Island, we went shopping at the Americana Manhasset, my materialistic safe haven. I love this mall. It is dripping with flashy unapologetic wealth that rivals a goddamn Jewels of Lalique exhibit at the Met. Anyway, we went to the Ralph Lauren store there so Dan could try on a tuxedo with his mom (she wanted to buy it for him, which I thought was sweet and awesome), but Dan gets so worked up when he's trying on clothes that I had to take a breather and go walk around. I stopped in Oliver Peoples and bought $300 sunglasses, but told everyone I got them at Top Shop to conceal my careless spending habits. Buying designer sunglasses was my "I need a drink" or even "I need to masturbate." It was a dirty little release. I can't watch Dan and his mom's dynamic for too long without needing a break. Or a shower. Your fiancé is probably not as anxious and definitely not the Son of Charlene, so your mileage may vary.

HAIR AND MAKEUP:
inconvenient truths

"BRIDAL HAIR" IS ITS OWN THING. IT'S *ROMANTIC* HAIR, WHICH is hair-larious because there is essentially nothing romantic about hair, except for when it's all messy because you just got laid. And sadly, nobody wants to see "she just got fucked!" hair at your wedding.

BIG BRIDAL SAYS: **Updos are classic and elegant.**

I SAY: **Yes, but they are not the only option.**

Tendrils, tendrils, so many tendrils. Wedding hair, no matter what year it is, is a real throwback to the days of using a curling iron, not to make beach waves or add texture, but to actually make curls, tight spirals, like those things that used to be a popular alternative to shoelaces in the early '90s.

If the bride clips in extra-long extensions, she will look like one of the princesses from *Bill & Ted's Excellent Adventure*. They were babes, yes, but you are not living in medieval times.

I will say, though, a lot of the newer, more trendy styles have a similar essence . . . they just throw a crown made of flowers on top and it's deemed "earthy." Or the bride will lean the other way and the hair will be intentionally disheveled, with leaves and twigs woven through it, like the bride was making out in the woods, but had to stop because she thought she saw a bear. Instead of taking a sec to comb the nature out of her head, she just ran straight to the altar.

As I do with everything else *re* weddings, I will embrace bridal beauty while ripping it a new bridehole. Everything is wonderful and stupid and beautiful and mockable. Do whatever you do for *you*. Because *you* love it.

Hairstyles

THE FROSE, AKA THE FROZEN ROSE

A high and tight bun, molded into the shape of a budding rose, using lots of bobby pins and even more hair spray.

PRO: This thing will stay put all night long. You might do the worm, but no garden critter will infiltrate this hard hair-sprayed garden.

CON: You have so many flowers at your venue. Do you need to construct one on your head? Granted, you don't have to water this one . . .

ALIEN MULLET

Bizarre updo that is more of a back-do, reaching into space behind you . . . where your hair has been sprayed, molded, or mounted into a shape so large and odd that the familiar contour of the human skull is indiscernible beneath it.

PRO: Your hair is so big, it will make the rest of you look teeny in comparison.

CON: Your new in-laws will wonder if your family has "come in peace."

THE "ADORN IN MY SIDE"

Any hairdo involving a tiara, a sparkle clip, headband, or tiny pinnable hat.

PRO: If your dress is relatively simple, with not a ton of bling, adorning your head can be a fun option for adding interest and complexity to your overall look.

CON: Accessories are extremely overwhelming. It's one more thing to think about, and they are not cheap. They are cheap—quality-wise—but not price-wise. Also, some of the headpieces and tiaras distract from the simple elegance of a bride. Also, no adult should wear a tiara. I mean you should, at your bachelorette as a joke, with plastic micro-shlongs stuck to it, but not the for-real kind with diamonds. If you pay more than a dollar for a tiara at a store other than Party City, I worry for you. UNLESS your wedding theme is JonBenét. (Whom I will keep mentioning; I have no shame.)

THE INDECISIVE

Half up, half down or lazily swept over one shoulder—like a low pony, but less straightforward.

PRO: It's not quite up, it's not quite down. Your hair is doing both/all. It's bi. You made a choice to not choose. And I'm pro-choiceless. This was my wedding hair, BTW, so I am a little biased . . . But I asked for it to look a little messy so from some angles it looks like I *had* a meticulously crafted curl heap, but then someone dumped catnip on it, and a cat came in and pawed at it, ate it a little, chewed at it a little.

BTW, I seriously hope Phoebe (pictured left) was tweeting, "I'm never getting married."

CON: The extensions needed to give this style fullness can be costly. Also, the look might not stay in place all night long, unless you decide not to dance at all. Great for boring brides!

TIP: If you get extensions, make sure they are dyed in advance to match your hair. Mine, revealed the day of, were three shades darker, and we had to not use them. Hundred and fifty bucks, gone. Couldn't return 'em.

Makeup Not Cake-Up

Just because you are getting married doesn't mean you have to wear a shit-ton of makeup. Yes, you want it to be a certain way for pictures, but if you're anything like me, having a ton of makeup on doesn't mean you feel more beautiful. If anything, you feel itchy (because who knows what's in that HD foundation), and like JonBenét. It's, like, "Hey, babe, you married me for me. Is it cool if I wear a mask, though?" When I showed my mom pictures from my makeup trial, she straight-up said, "You look ridiculous." I was offended at first, but ultimately agreed. I did look ridiculous. With the insectlike lashes and mauve shadow on my eyes and pearlescent browbones . . . It wasn't a classy look. But so much of your look you are "doing for the pictures." Everything is about the pictures! The pictures! And there is no focus on, simply, you looking crayyy in person, with aggressive stripes of bronzer under your cheeks, like Tony the Contour Tiger. But a good makeup artist will understand the balance between "doing it for the pics" and "doing it for the *now*."

 *I vow to look like myself at my wedding, not Maid Marian or Tammy Faye Baker.*

During the Wedding

IT TOOK SEVEN THOUSAND (REALLY) PHOTOS TO GET THIS
ONE REALLY SWEET ONE OF MY DAD AND ME.

WEDDING PHOTOGRAPHY
is fucking weird

SOME OF THE TRENDS IN WEDDING PHOTOGRAPHY NEED TO BE called out. It's one thing for a photographer to snap a candid of the bride fixing her father's tie—a tender, one-of-a-kind moment . . .

But some wedding photos border on (a) voyeurism and (b) time-filling-while-the-bride-is-busy nonsense.

> BIG BRIDAL: **Give your photographer a shot list!**
>
> I SAY: **A good photographer will get names of family and the bridal party in advance, but the pictures they take before the posed pictures are truly out of your control. And they will often reflect the photographer's "artistic sensibility."**

Let me break down the "classic" shots that most photographers seem convinced are essential, and what mine turned out like.

RINGS ON AN ADVENTURE

You know the shot: Super close up, the rings on top of the wedding program or hanging out on some country fence post. In my case, the rings were flanking G sharp. They're like Tom Hanks and his boss in *Big*, playing "Chopsticks" with their feet at FAO Schwartz. I didn't even realize there was a grand piano in my hotel suite until I got these pictures back and saw this. Note: I do not know how to play the piano, and neither does Dan. It has literally zero symbolism in our relationship. My grandma used to play, so maybe I can find meaning there? It's a stretch.

THE DRESS ON THE HANGER SHOT, I.E., DRESS SUICIDE, I.E., DRESSICIDE

For some reason, everyone gets the shot of the dress hanging on its (typically personalized) hanger. My photographer really took it up a notch. It looks like my dress and shoes were sick of my attitude, couldn't take being altered time and time again to fit my dumb weight-losing bridal body, and just gave up and hanged themselves from the middle of my hotel suite. They didn't even leave a note!

It also reminds me of when Gina Davis started to wither and crumble in her wedding dress in *Beetlejuice*. All dress, no human to fill it out. It's unsettling.

And last, but not least, my favorite of the trends . . .

THE PEEPING TOM

I feel like the photographers really swipe their creep card with this one.

Look at this arguably criminal photo. Note the darkened "vignette" corners he added to give the viewer the feeling of peering into a keyhole, jerking it to my Spanx? And speaking of darkened corners, the shadow on the shapewear creates the illusion of a cavernous anus, which appears to be almost the exact central point of the photo.

I understand that getting into your dress feels like a big moment before you get married, or to a photographer who likes taking pictures of butts and needs a reason to do so, but I am here to tell you: *Getting into your dress the day of your wedding is not a big deal.* You've done it a bunch already when you went to try it on, had a second fitting, then a third fitting . . . You and the dress are well-acquainted by the time your wedding rolls around.

Going back through my photos, there were several Peeping Tom shots that made me think, "Did the photographer really believe I would want these? Or did he just need a viable reason to be in the room while I changed?"

Like this one, me adjusting my dress, staring down at my boobs, like, "Oh, hey there, old pals. Let's do this."

Or the one below, where Erin is adjusting her boobs, I'm rocking a pair of super attractive girdle shorts in the background, and our photographer is just snap-snap-snapping away in the mirror. "They're going to want to remember this."

Word to the wise Khalifahs: Before sending a link to your online album around to friends—make sure you are comfortable with those friends seeing *all* of the pics.

Here is one photo you won't regret getting. You and your gal squad. I call this shot The Love Panini™. It's just special and reaffirming to physically see yourself sandwiched in between people you admire and cherish, who made the day so much better than it would have been without them. Before the wedding, I was fixated on how eight was an even number, and would allow for four girls on either side of me, versus three on one side and four on the other. "Won't it look weird in photos?!" Now all I see is seven people who enhance my life. That's a lot, pre-wedding Jamie. Be grateful.

I vow to laugh at wedding photography because 99 percent of it is questionable.

SOCIAL MEDEA: sorceress of envy

HERE'S A CURVE BALL: I DON'T THINK YOUR WEDDING HASHTAG *needs* to be funny or punny. It *can* be, by all means, if your husband's or wife's last name is Evans and you are dying for your hashtag to be #Evans ToBetsy or #ThankEvansIFoundHer. Here's the drawback: Those last name puns are usually already taken OR they could be taken at a later date, by someone else with your last name, which means your hashtag might just be yours now, but in a few years, it could get infiltrated by some hard-core Disney wedding with guests wearing mouse ears and the bride dressed as Belle from *Beauty and the Beast*. Great movie, but a mustard-yellow dress? And will the groom be in a full mask or will his natural appearance read as Beast?

> **BIG BRIDAL:** Make sure to post your hashtag on your wedding invitations and any wedding-related paper!
>
> **I SAY:** Or just figure out your hashtag close to the wedding and e-mail it to people. Maybe post it on a few signs that can then be scattered around the venue.

Also, not all last names lend themselves to great hashtag punning. Dan's last name is Black. I thought about #OnceJamieGoesBlack, I did. But . . . well . . . Moving on.

In the end, I went with #JamDan2016. I am glad I blended our names and added a number because while it's not funny, it's more like a computer password, which means it is less likely to be copied by someone else.

If you Bennifer your names together, it is a fun thing you can take with you throughout your marriage. I am pro-Bennifering and think it's a solid way of debuting your new identity as a unit, both at the wedding and going forward. Case in point: Just this week I sent an e-mail to friends for a get-together at my house and the subject head was "Brunch at Chez JamDan?" We still use our hashtag, kinda. It's fun.

Another thought: No sentence-long hashtags. I understand that if you start to input a hashtag on Instagram, it will automatically pop up after enough characters have been entered. Still though. Let's not. I saw one that was honestly like #WeArePeopleWhoAreHappilyMarried. If you want to write a memoir, don't do it in your hashtag. Clean, simple, original. Those are the requirements. #done.

I vow to value practicality over wit when choosing a hashtag.

ENFORCING
rules

CEREMONIES ARE THE SERIOUS PART OF THE WEDDING.
Everyone in the crowd is tense with excitement and fear. *Will the groom show up? Will their vows be sweet or embarrassing? Will the couple seem genuinely in love, or just moderately in love, or not at all in love?* The stakes feel high. If a baby in the crowd so much as giggles during the vow exchange, get ready for an army of heads to turn, collectively judging the mother who didn't put a tiny Hannibal Lecter mask on the little squishy time bomb to shush him or her. People are on edge.

> **BIG BRIDAL SAYS: Ask people to turn off their phones
> or even put them in a basket so they can enjoy the
> present moment that is your wedding.**
>
> **I SAY: I am not cruel.**

"Please turn off your phones." How about . . . Please turn on my interest? "There is no past. There is no future. Only us. Right now. The two worst people you've ever met."

I personally don't agree with this ask because, unless someone is such a dumb slug that they default to being bored and in need of constant phone stimulation, they're going to pay attention when you are up there at the altar. And if they're not paying attention, maybe it's because your ceremony is actually quite dull or long, or long and dull, in which case you should want them to be on their phones: If you can't give them a great show at least you are giving them the gift of distraction! We're all just terrible two-year-olds at a dinner party in need of an iPad to shut us up. As long as their ringer is silenced, why care? You won't even be looking at them.

They are just a sea of faces. Your officiant might ask you to "look at the people who love you" at the top of the ceremony. But after those glances are exchanged, after you "eye cheers" with everyone, you'll be back to staring at your partner. You will be more in the moment than you've ever been. If Eckhart Tolle, author of *The Power of Now,* were a guest, he'd gaze upon you and nod in appreciation. So let your guests tweet about the fact that the peacocks in the apiary are making weird mating noises. (Speaking from personal experience much?)

I vow to not take distractions personally. It's impossible to control or demand complete silence from a crowd of individuals.

THE FREUDIAN CLINCH OR
"you are my sunshine"

MAYBE SOMETHING IS WRONG WITH ME, BUT ALL OF THE father-daughter shit at weddings grosses me out, especially the father-daughter dance. It has a romantic quality of "Let's dance our last dance, shall we?" like you and your parent are lovers about to part ways.

Sexual implications aside, just because you are getting married doesn't mean you're parting ways, or that they stop being your parents. Really, they haven't PARENTED you in YEARS, so bringing them back in like they're still responsible for you just doesn't feel true to the story.

Also, the "last dance" tradition seems to further feed into that idea of the parent giving the child away. You are not property. This is not *Braveheart* where the dad hands his daughter off to an old merchant and then is hung in public or whatever the hell happened back then in *Braveheart* times. You sell your wife in exchange for a large goat that will feed the whole family for three weeks? I can't remember. All I know is, Mel Gibson hates Jews.

The reason this whole thing creeps me out is because there seems to be a subtle implication that your dad was your "first love." You may love him, but he was NOT your first love. He was never in that pool of men in your life. Nobody ever goes, "I love James now, before him, my college boyfriend, before him, Leo from next door, and, of course, Papa." NO! Who is yearning to be pelvis-to-pelvis with their father in a slow dance?? Who, I ask? And Dan dancing with his mom will always pose a problem for me.

There have been several instances over the past few years where I felt like Dan's mom was a little too involved in his life because, well, it's true that Jewish moms want to fuck their sons. Obviously, they don't *actually* want to—I am dialing up the hyperbole for comedic observational purposes—but that is a stereotype I've heard before, and all I am saying is, I see why. There is some kind of deep psychology at play there.

I first met Dan's mom when I went to Dan's brother's house for a BBQ by the pool. Dan took off his shirt and his mom went over to him and rubbed thick white sunblock all over his chest and back while he stood with his arms out like Jesus on the cross, enjoying the rubdown. I wanted to DIE. I wanted to be, like, "Lady, either give me the sunblock to put on him or HE WILL JUST HAVE TO BURN."

Another time, I was waiting next to the grill for some chicken to finish cooking. Dan's mom came up and said, "You can share some of my chicken." I was, like, "Nah, I'll just wait, thanks. Mine is almost ready." She pushes, "Jamie, come on, share the chicken." I go, "No, thanks," Third time, "Jamie, you sleep with my son, we can share some chicken!"

I was mortified. The fact that she mentioned her son sexually to me was a real "Say what?" moment. She was being funny, and I laughed, because she's truly hilarious, but I also thought, "She thinks about her son having sex."

Point is . . . I didn't need to see Dan and his mom and their relationship center stage at my wedding. It would just be an opportunity for her to whisper in his ear, "It should have been me . . ." I'm on the sideline waving like a dope, "Hi guys!!! Can I get my husband back or . . . No? Just going to keep swaying in each other's embrace? Cool. I'll just do some ayahuasca to deal with this trauma."

Not knowing how Freudian principles play out in your family, I'd encourage you to follow the wisdom of your heart and a trained clinician in making choices about dances.

FLAWS
will be flyin'

MY CEREMONY WAS MY FAVORITE PART OF MY WEDDING. BUT it was also the biggest clusterfuck. If I wasn't a stand-up comedian, looking at life through the somewhat permanent lens of "This will be good material!," I might be depressed about how it went down. Luckily, not only can I enjoy the shit-showiness of it all, I'm happy to relive it with you now.

Let's back up to a few hours before the ceremony, while we were at the hotel, taking pictures. Because the wedding planner was not there to wrangle and corral everyone in our group, around 3:00 P.M., I went from "Hope we are running on schedule!" to heart-palpitating irrational panic that I was going to be super late to my own wedding. I knew we had a hard out at 11:00 P.M., with the bar closing at 10:30 P.M., so I was dead set on starting at 5:30 on the dot to maximize our partying time. At the onset of the freak-out, I mentioned the timeline to my photographer, who assured me we were fine on time, but I didn't believe him. Next, I asked my bridesmaid Mary, and she assured me we were fine on time. I didn't believe her. This neurotic behavior continued until I got to the venue and did a champagne toast with my bridesmaids and parents in my little pre-wedding trailer (yes, in a trailer, like the kind meth heads live in, but with flowers and throw pillows instead of beakers) with a full twenty minutes to spare.

Then on to the ceremony! First of all, I started crying well before I walked down the aisle. I think part of me cried out of joy, out of overwhelming emotion, but also a little out of trepidation and embarrassment. I was scared to say my vows—was scared how they would come across to Dan and to everyone in the crowd. I was also fearful that my mom wasn't enjoying the moment fully. She is more cynical than I am (if that's possible), so there was part of me that kept thinking, "I hope she's enjoying herself and allowing herself to feel the feelings, even if they feel cheesy or sappy. I hope she just feels them."

Overall, I was embarrassed because the level of attention on myself in that moment, it didn't feel earned, it felt orchestrated. I am used to getting attention when I work for it, when I tell jokes on stage and people laugh in return. I'm used to "Sing for your supper" attention. "Entertain and you shall receive validation!" But bridal attention is different. You have coordinated for everyone to be in the room and put their focus on you. Of course they are happy to be there, of course they want to be there (or most do), but it still feels #weddiculous.

My wedding planner, upon seeing the tears form in my eyes, tried to stop me from crying. Which made me cry more? It was like we were having sex and I was about to finish and she was, like, "Don't finish, don't finish!!!!" but I couldn't help it. She was essentially telling my eyes not to cum. She recited a speech to me that clearly was her "Don't cry speech" that she gives every bride. I can't remember what it was, but she got very serious, and I just remember it feeling like a script, a spiel, that she's given to many a bride before me. I was waiting for her to say, "There's no crying in baseball." I guess she was worried I was going to ruin my makeup, but it's called waterproof mascara, bitch. I just remember being, like, "Get out of my face. It's my wedding, and I'll cry if I want to."

Before I walked down the aisle, my parents and I were waiting behind a row of bushes. I turned to my dad and said, "How are you feeling right now, Dad?" and he smiled like he was high—an ear-to-ear grin, like he had just ripped a bong hit and finished coughing and was now just feeeeel-ing it—and said, "Numb." (This is actually one of my favorite memories from my wedding day.)

That was the quiet before the storm . . . or drones. They were circling, buzzing about, like flies the size of Corgis. And I didn't have a giant swat-ter with me. Dan's dad and brother told me we would have one drone. It would cover the ceremony and then do a single pass over the reception while everyone was dancing. We wouldn't even notice, they said. But it's hard not to notice when you feel like you're under attack during a cere-mony where everyone is silent, watching you say some of the most im-portant words you'll ever say. The drones were like robotic wedding crashers . . . with wings. I feel like there were at least four looming. Maybe it was just one, but it felt like four. My friend Pete said at one point during the ceremony the drone flew right past his face, and he almost screamed because he thought it was a HAWK!

During our rehearsal, it was decided that my parents and Dan's par-ents would stand up under the chuppah with us, Dan's behind him, mine behind me. So throughout the ceremony there was the weird thing of me looking into Dan's eyes, but if my eyes moved at all, they would land on Charlene. So even when it was supposed to be just Dan and me, Charlene's positioning screamed, "And me!"

Our rabbi's singing voice was terrible. I had no idea. She had sere-naded us at the coffee shop meeting, and while awkward, her voice was decent. But I guess when she projects, she loses control . . . ? She sounded insane, like someone was stepping on the throat of a dying pelican. And she was supposed to just sing Hebrew after Shebbles read the English translation, but at one point she just started singing the English? So much not-previously-agreed-upon singing.

Next up (speaking of dying birds), there were actual birds making noises in the guest welcome area. They were not just chirping. They must have been mating. Deep, guttural cries of pleasure or pain . . . or the pleasure *of* pain. It was loud.

Oh yeah: Dan's nephews screamed within five seconds of me being up at the chuppah. It was an immediate, "I told you so."

When we broke the glass, Nicki Minaj's "I'm the Best" was supposed to be cued up and ready to drop the moment after the smash. Dan and I stood there, holding our hands in the air, waiting to exit, and there was a very pregnant pause because whoever was manning the iPod was just not on top of their shit. It was awkward, and very annoying. How many e-mails can you send, how many verbal confirmations can you get promising that they're on top of it? No amount of "Do you have it figured out? Everything good to go?" will make anything ever fully "good to go." Thank God for our vows. They were powerful, and grounding, and they made me appreciate the moment versus feel vexed by birds and rabbis who sound like birds.

Whatever happens day of, let it slide. So many things have been difficult along the way, why let another petty snafu make its way into your bank of stress? Don't make that deposit. You HAVE to laugh at the flaws, it's the only way to cope.

SEX ON YOUR WEDDING NIGHT:
the worst tradition

IT IS COMPLETELY UNFAIR TO EXPECT SOMEONE TO GET MADE up all day, take photos, say vows, party hard, after-party hard, and then still be down to plow.

Honestly, anyone who is eager to have sex on their wedding night is probably a serial killer with a bridal fetish, planning this evening for a long time. Post-wedding brunch? You won't be there, but the FBI will. At our after-party, I remember hitting a wall: I was just *done*. Needed to sleep, was enjoying the sliders Dan had ordered (Note: This was the after-party. We didn't serve them for dinner at the reception. See page 161.), had eaten four of them, and a pizza slice, three slices actually, and was just ready to crash.

Dan was having issues flagging down a waitress to come close out his tab and my patience was running out. Then Dan's groomsman Deacon said, "I'll take care of the tab, bro. Go bang your wife!" He's adorably abrasive . . .

When he said that, I smiled with tight-closed teeth and said, "Thanks, Deacon." The only thing I wanted to bang was my head against a steel pole because where was this fucking waitress?

We left Deacon to settle the bill and headed back to The Villa—my two-story hotel palace for one night only—and climbed into bed: The plushest mattress, the bajillion thread count sheets, and puffy pillows enveloped us like we were two bodies in a super comfy couple's coffin, and we sank into the comfort of that moment . . . the day is over. We turned on the TV and for some reason the only channel we could get was FOX News. And, believe me, nothing gets two newlyweds riled up and frisky like HD close-ups of dyed-blond pundits wearing foundation that doesn't match their faces, fired up about Hillary. I won't get into graphic detail about what happened next because . . . there isn't any! It literally went down like this:

> **DAN:** "Should we have sex?"
>
> **JAMIE:** "Can I just lay here and you just do it to me?"
>
> **DAN:** "Fuzz, we have to do it. It's tradition."
>
> **JAMIE:** "Is it rape if it's consensual, but I'm just not conscious?"

Dan laughed at my exaggeration, and an abbreviated mounting session commenced. I didn't have an orgasm. I didn't even want one. You know when you're so tired that the pressure to have an orgasm feels as taxing as putting together your gym bag and driving to the gym and parking and then you have to *still* work out?

It was a box to check off, and my box got checked. *Ew.* Sorry.

Now I know what they mean by "married sex." What it should be called is "exhausted newly married sex." Who has the energy to perform like a boundless unbridled horse after a day of go go go? My vagina doesn't need stimulation. The whole day was an orgasm. And, this may come as a surprise, but I'm not Sting. I'm not a Kama Sutra-rific climax factory. I'm just Jamie Lee: Basic Bitch. Newlywed. Tired.

WAYS TO TAKE THE PRESSURE OFF THE WEDDING NIGHT:

- **Have sex the morning of your wedding.** Yes, even though you're not supposed to see each other, do it early, before you are drained of energy and interest. Have your fiancé's groomsman put a bag over your fiancé's head and walk him to your room, marching him across the hotel property in total darkness like he's on death row in a third-world country. Turn off all the lights in your suite—bag over your own head is optional—and have your bridesmaid guide you to the bed, and then when the groomsman drops off your fiancé, he can leave with the bridesmaid . . . and if they're both single, maybe this bizarrely orchestrated fantasy will in some way get them in the mood. Then they'll go bone! I know what you're thinking: "Jamie is a goddamn sex counseling genius." It's true.

- **Phone sex.** This counts, right? Mutual masturbation before hair and makeup. Before coffee even? It's not intercourse, but who cares. Isn't the whole point—unless you're insanely religious and/or a virgin—to just prove that you still like each other after all these years? Or am I a deeply disturbed, jaded lady?

- **For the even lazier . . . sext throughout the wedding day.** I actually love this option. You and your man can start a chain early in the day where all you do is text filth to each other. It might not amount to actual between-the-sheets filth later on (Read: YOU WILL BE EXHAUSTED) but at least you can prove to yourself that even though you are married, you can still be adventurous sex heathens—which truthfully feels more significant than that familiar *mish posish* (missionary position) you assume however often you guys get down to . . . assuming. CATCH-22: If you designate someone to be in charge of your phone, just prepare them for groom dick pics popping up on the screen. #MoreLikeNUBtials.

After the Wedding

BEST DAY
of y'life

MY WEDDING WAS AMAZING—I WOULD NOT HAVE DONE ANYTHING differently—not because everything was perfect, but because whatever it was, it just WAS. *Wherever your wedding goes, there it went.* There's only so much you can control, and if you have that concept under control, you'll be thrilled with the outcome. You will still have strange remnants of feelings and resentment towards the process, but they will fade over time. Not all the way, but like stretch marks: You'll have them, but they won't be as red in five years. Time is your Mederma cream . . .

So yes, it's a nice day, there are a lot of lovely moments peppered in, but more than anything it is a complicated day. In many ways, it has the essence of a corporate workday, with a strict itinerary and deadlines: Hair and makeup must be finished by THIS time, photographs must be started at THIS time, everyone must get to the venue at THIS time . . . Even though my wedding coordinator was at the venue, she was not by my side while I was getting ready . . . so keeping things moving did fall on me.

IT WILL BE A TOP #1 DAY IF YOU ENJOY:

- Having makeup put on you for three-plus hours.

- Feeling needed—not in a romantic way, but in an "on the job" way. "You can't take off that day, we are understaffed." That kind of needing.

- Worrying that everyone is getting along okay.

- Worrying that you are in fact on schedule.

- Feeling responsible for everyone's health, happiness, appetite levels.

- Being barked at by a photographer wearing a matching Gucci belt and Gucci fanny pack to "act like you like each other!" and other corny jokes.

- Telling your makeup girl to mix three different lipstick colors because there isn't one in her giant kit that meets your needs because you are BEING FUCKING CRAZY.

- Realizing that weddings are in fact a circus without the fun of trapeze stunts and clowns scaring children . . . and that all the prep leading up to it has very little to do with your future husband and even less to do with your marriage.

- Hearing that your soon-to-be husband is upset in his hotel room because he needs . . . envelopes? There were no details given. He was just angry because he needed envelopes and didn't have them.

Leading up to your wedding day, you envision it like a Hollywood movie that you're going to be the star of, everyone waiting on you hand and foot so you can just relax because you are Cameron Diaz. But on the day it's less of a Hollywood movie and more a of a low-budget school play; you are the writer and creator of the play, you wrote it as a vehicle for you to star in, you felt the need to write it to communicate your truth, and even though you've hired friends to help with the production, hired your dad to go get craft services for the girls, hired a maid of honor to tell you that the extensions your hair girl brought are way too dark and you need to remove them, it's on you to pull off the play—you are not exempt. It's not a spa day for you, people need you or the show will not go on.

The truth is, there is no such thing as an uninterrupted twenty-four hours of bliss. Moments of bliss occurring throughout a twenty-four-hour period is a reasonable request. But a full day of sustained perfection is not realistic because, unfortunately, your wedding day still takes place on Earth. You can rent out an awesome venue, but, sorry, you cannot rent a unicorn-inhabited planet of rainbows and giggly pixies where hate and pain don't exist. Your wedding takes place here, on this messy, gritty planet, where your excitement and happiness ebb and flow, ranging from euphoric to annoyed to really annoyed to "Who the fuck put bluegrass on the Getting Ready playlist?!" If you see cracks in the stucco, don't panic. That's just life giving you a reality check, keeping you grounded, reminding you to take it all in. Honestly, thank God for the flaws of your wedding day—it snaps you back to Earth and makes you see what is in front of you. It would be a blur otherwise. A bridesmaid *should* rip her dress or get irritable with the makeup artist for not doing her cat eye "catty" enough. Whatever it is, it's just life being life.

Even if there is a "best day" of your life, you likely can't devise it. No amount of money or planning or centerpieces can replace an organic beautiful synchronicity that just . . . happens. For example: Dan and I took a road trip down the PCH after we got engaged and stopped in Carmel, California, a quaint, precious little town where we popped into tiny shops. (I'm very British in that way. I love small shops that you don't go in, you "pop into" . . . the kinda shops that have, like, eight candles, four tiny necklaces, and one $85 sweatshirt covered in splatter paint that you just HAVE to have.) After we walked around, we went to a golf course that had an outdoor bar and ordered boozy hot chocolates and watched the sunset. It was freezing, and they put out blankets for everyone to wrap up in. It was heaven. Earlier that day, Dan lost my favorite jacket. He put it down to take a photo of me on a rock and then left it on said rock. I wanted to kill him. I bought that jacket in London!!! Again, I am VERY British!!!!!! Anyway, did the jacket death overshadow the hot chocolate birth? Hell no. It was still one of the best days of my life. THIS is how we should view wedding days. Shit going wrong does not change the fact that everyone you love is in the same room. Done. Bye. Shut up. Enjoy it.

Also, the wedding actually starts a week before. The anticipation leading up to the wedding is a great place to mine "best moments." You are so busy looking forward that you never stop to enjoy the right-then. And you should because, basically, two weeks before your wedding is when you slowly start ramping up into full-blown euphoria. For me, the euphoria started kicking in the Saturday before my wedding when my mom and I were filling the gift bags for the hotel guests. It was a big chore—took over two hours, which I did not anticipate.

Dropping water bottles and packs of almonds and hair ties from Etsy that said "To Have And To Hold Your Hair Back" into bags, filling said bags with two types of tissue paper, gold and light pink, and then light pink and burgundy because I ran out of gold . . . It was oddly draining. But there was something fun about completing the task with my mom. The two of us have a history of crafting together. One time, we entered a corn dog art contest together. It was this weird festival/competition where you had to use corn dogs to make dioramas. I made one called "The Corbie Doll." I used flesh-colored clay to plump out a Barbie doll, covered her face in corn dog breading, and my mom helped hot glue a miniature corn dog to her hand. Anyway, point is, working on the gift bags felt like a throwback to our corn dog days. And that's when the nostalgia, and in turn the euphoria, began.

The euphoria grew in intensity the Thursday night before my wedding, when a lot of my family and Dan's family had arrived at the hotel.

My best friend, Erin, was there, and Bonnie, my other best friend, arrived with her husband, baby, and parents. The party hadn't officially started. It was the pre-party. We all met up at Bogies, a big outdoor lounge at Westlake Village Inn adorned with fire pits and plenty of heaters, giving it a cozy, snuggly bonfire kinda feel. We all met up there—not even at a specific time. It was like, "Come there if you want to hang. Or don't. The festivities don't officially start until tomorrow." That lack of pressure made everyone show up, and we had this effortless, relaxed great time. I looked around and caught glimpses of everyone just mingling and eating fried calamari and laughing. I saw my grandpa talking to Dan's little nephew, making him laugh the way my grandpa made me laugh when I was a wee one. I saw my brother-in-law talk to Bonnie's mom because they both work for KPMG and bonded over that. I saw my dad talking to Dan's dad. Everyone was illuminated by the fire. It was just the best. And zero planning went into it other than a group text that said, "Meet at Bogies?"

Instead of aiming to have the best day of your life, shoot for the best "week" of your life. It's actually easier and doesn't require every moment to be flawless. If you can, try to schedule other activities that are low-key where you can hang out with people: You don't even have to pay for them, just meet at a park or the bar in your hotel or the breakfast room at your Hampton Inn. Just try to socialize outside of the wedding. There is less pressure to look a certain way, feel a certain way, lift your chin for the camera a certain way. And a rehearsal dinner won't cut it. It needs to be an undemanding meet-up with no speeches. It's just about assembling people. Because here's the thing: Weddings are not unique. You have been to weddings; your guests have been to weddings. A wedding, itself, is a repeat experience. But having access to everyone in your life who matters at the same time is a one-of-a-kind experience. Milk it.

Also, try hanging out with guests one-on-one. Don't be afraid to stroll along the highway to a nearby Target with a pal to just do a lap, stare at cheap earrings that frankly should be cheaper because Target apparently doesn't know it's Target . . . Doesn't even have to be a top-tier wedding party friend or relative. It can be someone you run into in the hotel parking lot who, truthfully, you and your fiancé were on the fence about inviting. C-List Susie, who only got invited because you guys worked at the same dilapidated water park in the summer of '97. You aren't abandoning the rest of the group; you are taking some time for yourself. And these one-on-one moments are much more memorable afterwards than "group hangs." The only thing you remember about a group hang is "We were all there." You don't retain much from a group hang—not like you do one-on-one where the conversation can go somewhere—the memory is as general as a group photo with everyone's arms around each other.

Funnymoon

WHETHER YOU AND THE HUBS CLIMB MACHU PICCHU TWO DAYS after "I do," or wait a year to do a road trip in a rented Hyundai hatchback to Dollywood, a honeymoon is a great chance to, well, take a vacay. Vacations are awesome, whether they are linked to your wedding or not. They require a lot of planning though, so adding that planning on top of your wedding planning might be more masochistic than chillin' in Christian Grey's bone-zone dungeon.

> **BIG BRIDAL SAYS:** Set aside time to organize your honeymoon because once the planning is over, you'll be so glad there's a trip on the other side.
>
> **I SAY:** Book a resort-based slackfest on TripAdvisor, then focus on a life-changing adventure later.

I still plan on taking a bigger honeymoon to Japan at a later date (TBDizzle), but the Tuesday after our wedding, Dan and I embarked on a minimoon, where we crammed tons of honey into as much moon as possible in four days, before I had to fly to NY for work.

We decided to do Cabo because it's (a) close to LA, but (b) you still need a passport so it feels hella exotic, ya'll, plus (c) every hotel offers an infinity pool, if not multiple. Done.

I picked our resort on TripAdvisor one night when I was in bed on my laptop, with five computer windows open—four windows devoted to choosing my "wedding wardrobe" (I had an irrational need to wear all new clothes the weeks before and after my wedding) and one for a post-wedding trip. I did this same thing the next three nights, like a little pre-sleep ritual, then finally entered my credit card information and booked the damn thing.

In the back of our taxi, curving through the streets of downtown Cabo, which was filled with spring-break bars—one in particular that had a giant stucco cow on top with an udder about two stories high—I didn't know what to make of the town. We started driving away from the water, which made me very nervous. I kept asking the driver, who was sent by the resort, if it was on the water and he kept saying it was, but I started panicking, thinking, "He has to say that! He works for the hotel!" I have bouts of illogical anxiety that make no sense and I have them often. It was on the water and it was lovely. Also, the entrance to the resort was a giant metal gate. It had to have been fifty feet tall, and once you pull in you drive down a dramatic tunnel, like in *Roger Rabbit*, and the tunnel spits you out at the most immaculate view of the ocean, with several resort employees hovering, waiting to serve you. Which sounds amazing, but is also uncomfortable.

I highly recommend that you *plan to stay put. Do not move.* When I got to the resort, I immediately thought, "Dan and I have to schedule activities!" I collected brochures from the concierge for boat tours, whale watching tours, horseback riding tours. Dan was like, "Jamie, just relax. Let's just drink by the pool." I couldn't listen. And I should have. Poor Dan booked a jet-skiing session one afternoon, and a kayaking tour the next day at 8:00 A.M., just to shut me up. They were both underwhelming in comparison to reading *The Girl on the Train* poolside while sipping on alcoholic frozen perfection.

Do not feel guilty for wanting to sit and drink and eat—repeat. You just planned a wedding. That's enough adventure for a while!

Except for sex. There will be pressure, again, to have sex, which brings me to . . . *rose petals on the sheets. They are strangely a turn-on, but also very messy.* When we got back from dinner the first night, there were candles lit all over the room, the maids had clearly turned up the stereo (didn't even know we had one in the room til this moment), and it was BLAST-ING Spanish guitar music, like we were in *Zoro*, like I was suddenly that dancing emoji in the red dress. There were sooooo many rose petals on the bed. Not a light spackling, but a dense membrane of red. I couldn't even see the white comforter underneath it.

And similar to the wedding night, I don't like being told when to have sex, I don't like mandated "This is do-it time" times. Dan and I just had a huge dinner, fish with mashed potatoes and mixed drinks, and my stomach was sticking out like I had just swallowed my zebra print airplane pillow. I was feeling GRUESOME. Plus, Dan and I are comedians so we're not the kind of people who listen to sensual Latin sex guitar music without laughing. In fact, before we got down (again, pressure), we got so stupid. I started drumming to the music, using my own butt as a drum kit, slapping my own cheeks, and Dan, well, he started playing his penis like a guitar. Suddenly, we were in Carlos Santana's twisted fantasy band. We literally "played" along to three whole songs—and they were long songs. We kept laughing and playing ourselves like instruments. Finally, we shtupped . . . and as you know, shtupping can be messy. No, not like that . . . There were stains! No, not like that!! ROSE PETAL STAINS. When we climbed out of bed, what was once a white comforter was now pink from flower stains.

Note: I share the story of our butt and penis band to highlight that what matters in the end, the best moments of your entire wedding journey, will likely be unexpected, unique to you and your partner, and something that you can't plan in advance. Then again . . . Bongos & the Penis Guitar are available for weddings.

MISC. reflections

MOJITO TIME. LET'S KICK BACK AND REFLECT. I SPENT A YEAR in a constant state of expectation, projecting how I wanted the wedding to be. I should at least spend a few minutes looking back.

Lies Others Told Me

There are so many notions flying around when you're planning your wedding. Here are some things people told me that I found to be untrue.

> **"ONCE YOU BOOK THE BIG STUFF LIKE THE BAND AND THE VENUE, YOU CAN RELAX."**

Not true. I was dealing with minutia all the way through. I had to buy a basket for flip-flops by the dance floor, and Dan was worried about whether the cocktail hour would have enough food, which made me worried. Our first photographer wanted a huge hunk of change to own all of our photos, so we had to switch photographers a month before the wedding. Then there're personal minutia: What level spray tan should I get? Should I skip the spray tan altogether so it doesn't come off on my white dress? (It doesn't by the way, as long as you don't get it the day before.)

What was I going to wear to the rehearsal dinner? What about the day before the rehearsal dinner? It was nonstop.

"THE WHOLE THING IS A BLUR."

Not true. I remember almost every detail of my experience. The only thing that makes it feel like a blur is that you can't possibly see everything that goes down at the wedding because you can't be at every table, alongside each and every guest at every moment, observing their experience. You are only one person; even though it is your wedding, that doesn't mean you get eyes in the back and sides of your head and another pair of eyes in the palms of your hands like that very rude *Pan's Labyrinth* monster. The upside to this lack of awareness is hearing stories from guests later . . . like how a few of my friends convinced a mutual friend, Shawn, that Bonnie was my surrogate, carrying Dan's and my child. Bonnie was pregnant, but with her own child. Shawn didn't find out the truth until the car ride home. The whole time he was at my wedding, he thought my matron of honor was knocked up with my child.

"FLOWERS ARE A WASTE OF MONEY WHEN YOU'RE GETTING MARRIED AT AN OUTDOOR VENUE THAT HAS NATURE ALL AROUND."

Having a little sumthin-sumthin on every table does add to ambiance. Nobody cares, nobody really notices it, but you will notice. It will add to *your* enjoyment.

"YOU FORMULATE A BUDGET, AND YOU STICK TO IT."

Be prepared to go over, and also be prepared for it to work out. I'm not saying money grows on trees, but with weddings, it kind of does—more than in regular life. If you go over, you will be okay. It will be stressful, it will feel overwhelming, but you'll work it out. My husband used to be an accountant. He's meticulous with money, and we still went over budget.

I felt relieved. No more planning! No more tension! Everyone had a blast! I felt tired and bummed/a little empty when saying good-bye to family members and friends, specifically my mom, my dad, Charlene, and Lenny. But I kept feeling high on love and excitement even after people left. It was all so wonderful, and the end of something doesn't negate the wonderfulness. To be clear, I have heard of Post-Wedding Depression, and I do think it is real and very valid. But! I think it is a result of something deeper; something more profound is going on if you feel truly depressed. Get help! Help helps!

Things That I Thought Would Matter That Actually Didn't

- Having a wedding website. People still text you questions, e-mail you questions; it's not a catchall for avoiding conversations about where you are registered.

- Cake topper: Who gives a shit? Have fun with it, have your mom make you one.

- Change of shoes: I immediately put on flip-flops after the hora.

Things That Surprised Me

- Flip-flop basket was a hit.

- People straight up don't show up, even if they RSVP'd "Will Attend!"

- You should think about the order in which you want your wedding party to walk down the aisle BEFORE rehearsal. I gave no thought to this, and the rehearsal was anarchic because of it. Who goes first, second, third, etc. is not a last-minute decision, so do not treat it as such.

Things I Could Have Done Without

I'm not using the word "regret" because it's a strong word and because I feel like the true definition of regret is something that haunts you later: You fucked up so hard it still crashes over you like a guilt tsunami one day while you're minding your own business . . . then the pang hits you. "I kissed my best friend's boyfriend when I was eighteen!" And then it fades, and you get the pang again every two months until one day you die. *These* here are things that I laugh at because what choice do I have? Can't redo the wedding.

- Making my parents worry about money: Coming up with it, wishing they could put in more. I wish I had paid for the whole thing.

- Arguing loudly with Dan in front of Dennis. He is a sensitive pooch.

- Not standing up for myself more clearly and directly to Dan's family. Not in a mean way, just in a calm "This is what I need to stay sane" way.

- Hiring the more experienced band over the cooler one.

- The level of religiousness, which apparently wasn't even that high. It just didn't reflect me. I was not raised religious. It is tough to feel emotionally connected to traditions you did not grow up with—no matter how much your partner connects to them.

Fears Now That I'm Married

I'M NERVOUS THAT . . .

- I now appear older. That I am put in a box of "older, more settled, less adventurous, less available to hang out."

- People will see me as less independent.

- People will expect us to have kids right away.

- I seem like less of my own person. What I do reflects on Dan, and what Dan does reflects on me, and we are seen as a unit.

- Now that we're married, is my money his money? Is his money my money? Is my love is your love is my love is your love? Yes, I'm quoting Whitney, you got me! But seriously, I am the current breadwinner, and I get scared that maybe he will feel less energized to make money because I am stable enough to support both of us at the moment. Should I suddenly work less to scale back and force his hand? We are not exactly a two-income household (I mean, technically we are, but not really), and I constantly feel pressure to keep bringing in the dough.

- Our wedding issues will come back around and haunt our marriage. Will Dan's mom always have more influence than I do?

BUT I'M EXCITED THAT . . .

- When you have a fight, you can't bail. You have to work it out, and the faster you work it out the faster you guys can just go do something fun like the best friends that you are, like eat brunch, or judge other couples even though you have no actual basis for judging . . .

- I get to be family with someone who is also my friend. When you are a little girl—especially as an only child like myself—all you want in the world is to have your best friend be your sister. "I wish we had the same DNA, dammit! We have such good Calico Critters chemistry, it sucks that we aren't just from the same family and that this other woman you call 'Mom' always comes to pick you up right when things are getting good." When you are married, it's the closest you get to being family with your friend. You don't share DNA, and you wouldn't want to because that would be incest, but you *do* share a joint account for vacations and list each other on tax forms!

- The power of an official married "we" gets you out of stuff more easily than an "I." If you have another person present when you are at a party, the two of you can cyclically blame one another for needing to leave. Nobody will ever challenge a "we." Single Darren wants to leave the party, single Kendra says, "Come on! It's only nine thirty!" But *we* (Dan and Jamie) want to leave? "Totally get it. Thanks for coming, guys!"

- One person's success benefits both. It's like a rock-climbing wall where as long as one hand moves up, a foot will follow and find one of those colorful clay pegs. You guys are one body, so it doesn't matter which hand or whose foot just as long as the weird two-headed rock-climbing beast is moving! In the same way I worry about being seen as a unit, the power of a unit, in success, can be more powerful than you on your own.

- You'll always have someone to fight with, which inevitably reflects your own weaknesses back at you, forcing you to confront everything you don't want to face about yourself. But then, in the presence of your partner, you actually grow as a person! It's brutal but necessary, like emotional wildfire that clears the forest floor of debris and lets more light in. And as a bonus, you get to be the wildfire to their flaws.

BRINGING UP
*mari**

WHEN I LIVED IN NEW YORK CITY, I WOULD OFTEN SEE
European tourists. A whole family: Mom, dad, and two children in their
late twenties. Everyone was holding hands and laughing and kissing. It
was a little gross, but also a lesson: They just like each other! They don't
fear closeness. Those "kids" probably even live with their parents still.
Who cares? Family isn't embarrassing over there the way it is in America.
In America, it's all about breaking away from the nest to prove you can
stand on your own two feet. When I think of an American dude living in
his parents' basement I think, "How sad." But when I think of a French
dude living in his parents' basement, I think, "I bet they have really fun
boisterous dinners together!" Try to apply this mind-set to weddings and
marriage. If you can rewire your brain to view all of the doubt-inducing
flare-ups along your path to the wedding—viewing family as "big, loud,
and funny" versus "detrimental, boundary-less, and hair-raising"—it
will help.

---

* "Husband" in French.

I read *Bringing Up Bébé*, which is all about how the French prioritize their marriage and sex life, and their lives in general, above their children's. Not in an abusive way, but in a balanced way. And Americans clearly sacrifice themselves to the point of no sex, losing their own identity, and putting their kids on an unhealthy pedestal.

This book was insanely helpful in realizing that American marriage is not the only way . . . Let's do as the French do: Eat bread, get skinny, fuck our husbands, have gorgeous skin even though we smoke a pack a day. I think this needs to be a movement. *Love the way the French love.* Granted, I haven't actually spent enough time in France to know what the hell I am talking about. I have been to Paris a few times and then once went to see the cave paintings in Northern France, and there was a ghost in our hotel. (She slept above me while I slept . . . Does this discredit me as your author? I'm sorry. But her presence was hella felt.)

My advice is: *Love like we THINK the French love.* Now when you get in an argument, it's not unfortunate, it's *passionate.* Now when your mother-in-law infiltrates your life, it's not annoying, it's *European-style closeness.*

Marriage: My Plant Theory

Big Bridal loves to separate the wedding from the marriage, to the point where we forget what weddings are really about. "Mason jars?" No. "Mason jars dipped in glitter?" No! Well, maybe . . . that sounds spunky. Culturally, we make weddings a symbol of the bride's identity, her party planning skills, her attention to detail, and her taste. The groom is a side business. I'm all for the bride calling the shots. But the complexity and day-to-day compromising and learning and growing that comes from *being in a marriage* is almost taboo to discuss or mention or ponder when you are engaged. We're supposed to just focus on flowers and turn off our brains when it comes to analyzing fears, questions, and paranoia. Sure, *The Knot* will suggest talking to a financial planner in certain articles, but that's about as real as they get. They would never straight-up give you a list of couple's counselors to reach out to in your area. Needing help or expressing concern or, dare I say *doubts,* is a sign of weakness, a sign of failure.

> BIG BRIDAL: **Now that you're married, we have literally nothing to offer on that subject matter. Please come see us when planning Wedding Number Two.**
>
> ME: **Oh *now* you're silent! I guess I'll look into my heart for that wisdom.**

I have a theory I'm working on and planning on using as I head into marriage. For humans in a relationship, you and your partner are the plant, the soil is your home (where you are planted: living together, absorbing each other's nutrients and toxins), and *life* is the sun (reminding you to enjoy each other because someday you'll die, so don't waste energy not being happy while you're here on this planet).

Life converts all the nutrients and toxins (fights, discussions, chats) into lessons of "What did we learn about each other, what do we mutually gain from each other, how can we grow together." And that gets fed back into the soil . . . your home, your base. That enriched soil feeds the plant, allowing it to grow and expand and triumph and maybe even make baby plants.

Oh, also, all of the appliances you get from your registry make the soil reallll nice and fertile. Our soil is undeniably improved now that I have a slow cooker and cold-brew maker. Oh, and a popsicle mold.

ACKNOWLEDGMENTS

I WOULD LIKE TO EXPRESS MY MOST SINCERE THANKS TO THE following people:

My husband. Thank you for taking care of me, for reminding me to eat, and for whipping up delicious food while I was hunched over my laptop, writing, neglecting any and all wifely duties.

My mom and dad. The most supportive, the most encouraging. Thank you for loving coffee as much as I do.

My aunts, uncles, cousins, and grandpa. I am lucky to know, and call family, such funny, smart, caring, cool people.

Dan's mom and dad. Love you guys. There are no two people I would rather hate LA with. Remember the unicyclist who wheeled in front of the car? Ugggh.

My grandma Eleanor. She passed away before I started writing this book, and I think if she had been around during the WPP, everything would have been easier and better. The world just isn't what it was without her.

Erin. You're a visionary. Plain and simple.

Bonnie, Margie, Shawlini, Phoebe, Diane, Giulia, Kate, Kara, Merrill, Beth. You made the whole "getting hitched" thang infinitely more special.

Neil, Mikey, and Erica. Thank you for your help and support during the wedding and the months leading up to it.

Leslie. Thank you for listening to me complain, and for making me look presentable. You are such a talent. And thanks for introducing me to Carrie. She's awesome.

Hilary at HarperOne and Anthony at Foundry. You are superstars.

Matt and David at Avalon. Thank you for making my life easier.

Jacqueline Novak. A partner, a genius, a friend.

Jesus. JK.

INDEX

10–12; Big Bridal is watching, 12–14; Decision Dump, 44; decision-making challenges, 41–44; doubts, 185–92; inkblot test to assess emotional capacity for, 11; process, 7–14; publications offering guidance, 6–7; reasons for reading book about, 4, 9–10; stress and, 181–84; wedding party characters involved in, 69–79

weddings: after, 253–70; art project approach, 17–18; average costs, 38; best day of life, 253–58; as blur, 263; budgets, 22, 25, 38–40, 263, 265; chill vibe, 49; as circus, 254; dates, 18, 42–43; during, 233–50; excited about, 266–67; fears now that I'm married, 265–66; as Hollywood movie, 254; lies others told me, 262–64; locale, 41–43, 198; making unforgettable, 160; memorable, 159; miscellaneous reflections, 262–67; natural disasters, 14, 156; night weddings, 163; not home, 122; popular time for, 47; reception, 22, 51; rehearsal, 246; seasons, 45–50; things I could have done without, 265; things that I thought would matter that actually didn't, 264; things that surprised me, 264; venues for, 22, 47, 51–56, 262; wedding favors, 158; wedding guides, 10; wedding programs, 27, 39

wedding websites: "About" section, 97–98; airport information, 99; including transparency about who is single, 99; reasons for having, 264; registry, 99; setting up, 95–98; things to include in addition to event details, 99

Wedding Wonderfuls!, 86

welcome bags, 27, 29

Westlake Village Inn, 257

white, 61

white(ish) dress, 225

wild boar, 145

wind, 48

winter weddings, 44, 46

Witherspoon, Reese, 37

worry, 254

Y

yoga, 181

JAMIE LEE is a stand-up comedian, TV writer, and actress, and one of the core cast members on the hit MTV show *Girl Code*, as well as the host of *10 Things* on truTV and the podcast *Best of the Worst*. Jamie has appeared on *Conan*, *Chelsea Lately*, *The Late Late Show with James Corden*, Comedy Central's *@Midnight*, MTV's *Ridiculousness*, and *John Oliver's New York Stand-Up Show*, and was a semi-finalist on *Last Comic Standing*. She has also written for *The Pete Holmes Show*, E!, Lifetime, TLC, and the new Judd Apatow show on HBO, *Crashing*. She lives in Los Angeles with her husband and a Labradoodle named Dennis. Visit her at www.jamieleecomedy.com.